D1352812

Howard A. Snyder

NEW WINESKINS

CHANGING THE MAN-MADE STRUCTURES OF THE CHURCH

MARSHALL, MORGAN AND SCOTT
LONDON

To my parents
Edmond C. Snyder
Clara Zahniser Snyder
who first taught me to love the church

MARSHALL, MORGAN AND SCOTT, *a member of the Pentos group*, 1 Bath Street, London EC1V 9LB. First published in the United States of America by Inter-Varsity Press 1975. First British edition Marshall, Morgan and Scott 1977. ISBN 0 551 05562 6. Printed in Great Britain by J. W. Arrowsmith Ltd, Bristol. 771070L50.

CONTENTS

ACKNOWLEDGMENTS

This book incorporates, in somewhat revised form, the following previously published articles by the author:

"The Fellowship of the Holy Spirit," Christianity Today, *15, No. 3 (November 6, 1970), 4-7. Copyright 1970, Christianity Today, Inc. Used by permission. "Church Renewal Through Small Groups."* United Evangelical Action, *30, No. 2 (Summer, 1971), 29-31. "Does the Church Suffer an 'Edifice Complex'?"* World Vision Magazine, *15, No. 8 (September, 1971), 4-5. Copyright 1971, World Vision, Inc. Used by permission. "The Gospel to the Poor."* United Evangelical Action, *30, No. 4 (Winter, 1971), 10-16. "A World Come Full Circle."* Christianity Today, *16, No. 7 (January 7, 1972), 9-13. Copyright 1972, Christianity Today, Inc. Used by permission. "John Wesley, A Man for Our Times."* Christianity Today, *16, No. 19 (June 23, 1972), 8-11. Copyright 1972, Christianity Today, Inc. Used by permission. " 'The People of God'–Implications for Church Structure."* Christianity Today, *17, No. 2 (October 27, 1972), 6-11. Copyright 1972, Christianity Today, Inc. Used by permission. "Should the Protestant Pastor be a Superstar?"* The Other Side, *9, No. 2 (March-April, 1973), 8-11. "Misunderstanding Spiritual Gifts."* Christianity Today, *18, No. 1 (October 12, 1973), 15-18. Copyright 1973, Christianity Today, Inc. Used by permission. "Do Christians Know Satan's Strategy for the Battle Now Being Fought?"* Light and Life, *107, No. 3 (February 19, 1974), 7-8.*

PREFACE

I publish this book at the close of six years of missionary service in São Paulo, Brazil. During this time my responsibilities have included seminary teaching and administration, pastoral work in two local churches and administrative tasks related to my mission.

Leaving the North American scene and becoming involved in the work of the church in another culture prompted me to a fundamental rethinking of the mission and structure of the church in today's world. Reading, reflection on my pastoral experience in Detroit, Michigan, my involvements in Brazil and, above all, direct Bible study have together brought me to the conclusions and (in some cases) hypotheses which I venture to set forth in this book. Particularly helpful was an intensive study of the book of Ephesians during 1971.

Some of this material has been previously published elsewhere, as indicated below. I wish here to thank the various publishers involved for making it possible for me, through this book, to present this material to a wider audience.

In July of 1974 I presented a paper entitled "The Church as God's Agent of Evangelism" at the International Congress on World Evangelization in Lausanne, Switzerland. Chapter 12 of this book incorporates some of the basic ideas and analyses from that paper. Portions of that paper have also been included in the "Reaching All" congress study guide series, particularly in the booklet, Reaching All Together. *These study guides are now available from World Wide Publications, 1313 Hennepin Avenue, Minneapolis, Minnesota 55403.*

The publication of this book owes much to many people. I would particularly like to thank Doug Smith and Laverne Blowers, missionary colleagues in Brazil, who read the book in typescript and offered helpful suggestions; and my wife, Janice, who helped with the proofreading and with encouragement.

INTRODUCTION: NEW WINE AND OLD WINESKINS

Frankly, I have never had much experience with either wine or wineskins—of the literal variety. But for several years I have been intrigued with Jesus' words in Luke 5:37-38: "No one puts new wine into old wineskins, for the new wine bursts the old skins, ruining the skins and spilling the wine. New wine must be put into new wineskins" (Living Bible).

What did Jesus mean? Certainly he did not mean everything that Christians through the years have taken from these words. Jesus distinguishes here between something essential and primary (the wine) and something secondary but also necessary and useful (the wineskins). Wineskins would be superfluous without the wine they were meant to hold.

This is vital for the everyday life of the church. There is that which is new and potent and essential—the gospel of Jesus Christ. And there is that which is secondary, subsidiary, man-made. These are the wineskins, and include traditions, structures and patterns of doing things which have grown up around the gospel. In this book I am particularly concerned with the *relationship* between such wineskins and the gospel wine, and with the question of *what kinds of wineskins* are most compatible with the gospel in modern techno-urban society. For the wineskins are the point of contact between the wine and the world. They are determined both by the wine's properties and the world's pressures. Wineskins result when the divine gospel touches human culture.

In the passage about wineskins in Luke 5, Jesus' critics come to him with a question: "Why do your disciples eat and drink, while John's disciples and those of the Pharisees fast and pray?"

Jesus first answers by speaking of the bridegroom. "Can you make wedding guests fast while the bridegroom is with them? The days will come when the bridegroom is taken away from them—then they will fast!" Jesus himself was the bridegroom, and while he was on earth with his disciples it was entirely appropriate for them to feast and make merry.

But Jesus does not stop there. He goes on to speak of new cloth and new wine. Jesus knew where the real problem was. He knew what was behind the question raised by the scribes and Pharisees. They were irritated because Jesus was not obeying all their traditions. They were really asking the same question they had raised in Matthew 15:2: "Why do your disciples transgress the tradition of the elders?"

So Jesus says, "No one tears a piece from a new garment and puts it upon an old garment; if he does, he will tear the new and the piece from the new will not match the old. And no one puts new wine into old wineskins; if he does, the new wine will burst the skins and it will be spilled, and the skins will be destroyed. But new wine must be put into fresh wineskins."

The last statement is the key: "New wine must be put into fresh wineskins." The old Judaism could not contain the new wine of the gospel of Christ. The Christian faith would have to grow and burst the old wineskins of Judaism. And that is what happened. The church began to spread into the whole world, shedding the old Jewish forms.

We learn two things here. First, this parable reminds us that God is always a God of *newness.* The gospel is new—always.

The Old Testament frequently speaks of new things. We read of a new song, a new heart, a new spirit, a new name, a new covenant, a new creation, a new heaven and a new earth.[1] David said, "[God] put a new song in my mouth" (Ps. 40:3). And we read other statements such as these:

"Behold, the former things have come to pass, and new things I now declare; before they spring forth I tell you of them" (Is. 42:9).

"Behold, I am doing a new thing; now it springs forth, do you not perceive it?" (Is. 43:19).

"And I will give them a new heart, and put a new spirit within them" (Ezek. 11:19).

"For behold, I create new heavens and a new earth" (Is. 65:17).

In the *New* Testament the gospel of Christ is similarly described. Hebrews 10:20 says that the gospel is "the new and living way." And Jesus said as he instituted the Lord's Supper, "This is my blood of the new covenant" (Mt. 26:28).

God is a God of newness. On the one hand he is the Ancient of Days, "the Father of lights with whom there is no variation or shadow due to change" (Jas. 1:17), and Jesus Christ is "the same yesterday and today and for ever" (Heb. 13:8). But this does not mean that God is static or stationary. The history of God's people in the Bible and the history of the Christian church show just the opposite. In every age the true biblical gospel is a message of newness and renewal.

God has not stopped doing new things. The Bible says, "We wait for new heavens and a new earth in which righteousness dwells" (2 Pet. 3:13). Many of the Old Testament prophecies already cited were fulfilled in part with the coming of Christ and the birth of the church, but the prophetic fund has not yet been exhausted. Unfulfilled prophecies and promises of new things remain. At the end of the Bible God is still saying, "Behold, I make all things new" (Rev. 21:5).

Every age knows the temptation to forget that the gospel is ever new. We try to contain the new wine of the gospel in old wineskins—outmoded traditions, obsolete philosophies, creaking institutions, old habits. But with time the old wine-skins begin to bind the gospel. Then they must burst, and the power of the gospel pour forth once more. Many times this has happened in the history of the church. Human nature wants to conserve, but the divine nature is to renew. It seems almost a law that things initially created to aid the gospel eventually become obstacles—old wineskins. Then God has to destroy or abandon them so that the gospel wine can renew man's world once again.

The gospel is new in our day. It is still "the power of God." It is still bursting old wineskins and flowing forth into the world. All I attempt to say in this book grows out of a deep confidence in Jesus Christ and in the renewing power of his gospel.

But there is something else this parable teaches us—the *necessity* of new wineskins. Wineskins are not eternal. As time passes they must be replaced—not because the gospel changes, but because the gospel itself demands and produces change! New wine must be put into new wineskins—not once-for-all, but repeatedly, periodically. This book is written to emphasize the relativity of church structures and to suggest some bases for the necessary updating of wineskins.

Four Modern Currents Four currents have been agitating much of the evangelical Protestant church for the past decade or so, producing ferment and change. I believe all of these have been used by the Holy Spirit, and I have incorporated insights from each into this book.

First is the Personal Evangelism Movement, that stream which has been calling Christians to renewed evangelistic and missionary endeavor to fulfill the Great Commission "in our generation." This movement has spawned several evangelistic organizations and sparked a host of books on evangelism. This is an essential emphasis, but it is a partial one; and in its zeal for evangelism the Personal Evangelism Movement has sometimes neglected the church and the question of church structure.

There is, second, the Church Renewal Movement. Numerous speakers and writers have emphasized that the church's life must be grounded in community, in biblical *koinonia*, or soul-fellowship. The small group has been rediscovered as a structure for community life. I see this emphasis also as necessary and biblical. But an exaggerated emphasis here can produce an unhealthy, subjectivistic, pulse-taking kind of Christian experience which is ingrown and fuzzy on doctrinal truth. Renewal and community are not ends in themselves.

A third stream is the Church Growth Movement. Sparked initially by Donald McGavran, it has now reached a level of remarkable sophistication and influence. Since the attention of this movement has been primarily directed toward foreign missions, many North American Christians in institutional churches have been largely untouched by it. As a missionary, I have had contact with and benefited from the Church Growth Movement, and bring some insights from it into my discussions in this book. While in essential agreement with the emphasis—which argues forcefully that Christian churches are divinely intended to grow significantly in number—I feel it also needs the corrective of other biblical emphases to keep it from turning into a mere "spiritual technology."

There is, finally, the Charismatic Movement, which strongly proclaims the immediacy of life in the Spirit and the exercise of spiritual gifts. I have no doubt that God has used this movement to restore to the church these needed and biblical accents. If the charismatics tend at times to be "divisive" or "too emotional" or "weak on doctrine," they also have gotten hold of some solid biblical truths the church needs.[2] I have benefited from this movement.

So evangelism, small groups, church growth and spiritual gifts all find their place in this book. But more than anything else, the ideas and insights presented here grow out of a continuing dialogue with the Word of God and with others who, like me, have been involved in a spiritual quest to rediscover the true, biblical church of Jesus Christ.

The Bible says the church is nothing less than the Body of Christ. It is the Bride of Christ (Rev. 21:9), the flock of God (1 Pet. 5:2), the living temple of the Holy Spirit (Eph. 2:21-22). Virtually all biblical figures for the church emphasize an essential, living, love relationship between Christ and the church. These figures underscore the overwhelming importance of the church in God's plan and remind us that "Christ loved the church and gave himself up for her" (Eph. 5:25). If the church is the Body of Christ—the means of the Head's action in the world—then the church is an essential part of the gospel, and ecclesiology is inseparable from soteriology. Those Christians who adopt what might be called an "antichurch stance" tamper with the very gospel itself, while at the same time demonstrating a misunderstanding of what the Bible means by *the church.*

The reader will soon discover that I have not attempted to give a detailed program for church structure. No overall blueprint for the church is proposed. Rather, I have tried to speak more basically about underlying principles and understandings that must shape any valid and biblical structure in our day. So this book is suggestive, not definitive. I have opened more doors than I have chosen (or been able) to enter. Several questions are dealt with only partially and incompletely, and thus form the agenda for future thought, study and writing. More detailed and systematic proposals for church structure can be found in some of the books cited in the notes and bibliography.

New wine must be put into new wineskins. But where do these wineskins come from? Who supplies them? How are they made? What determines their usefulness? This book seeks to answer such questions.

1

THE IMPOSSIBLE CATACLYSM

It is hard to escape the conclusion that today one of the greatest roadblocks to the gospel of Jesus Christ is the institutional church. The student protester who held up a placard "Jesus Yes! Christianity No!" was expressing a sentiment widely felt: The institutional church too often represents something radically different from the Jesus Christ of the Bible.

But how can one get at Christ if not through the church? And how can the church present Jesus without itself getting in the way? In our fast-changing world fewer and fewer people are interested in a pile of old wineskins, no matter how well-preserved they may be.

The situation today is not without its ironic humor. On the one hand, much of the institutionalized church talks to itself in a corner about how to be relevant and usually comes up with a theology that has as its unstated premise, "If you can't beat 'em, join 'em." Too often it presents a "theology" of political and/or social involvement so hopelessly tied to its historical-cultural context that its demise precedes that of its promoters.

Meanwhile, back at the TV screen, the youth of today are on center stage telling us to junk the church and give them *experience*—"something to feel in the stomach." They do not want a theology to believe or even a cause to live for but first of all an experience of something ultimately real. Their enchantment with drugs or oriental mysticism or the Guru Maharaj Ji is really an acted-out parable. It says, "Give us a taste of experience."

We *could* do this. The church could present Christ, not an institution or a theology or a program. The church could present Jesus, not an antiquated and adulterated Christianity. But of course it doesn't. It tries to brew a new wine instead of scrapping the old wineskins.[1]

I think of Gibson Winter's *The Suburban Captivity of the Churches,* Peter Berger's *The Noise of Solemn Assemblies,* H. Richard Niebuhr's *Social Sources of Denominationalism,* Harvey Cox's *The Secular City* and similar books. While often incomplete in their analysis and unsound in their solutions, yet taken together such books present a devastating criticism of American Protestantism. They show that the American Protestant church is not only *in* the world; it is, to a large degree, also *of* the world.

I write as an evangelical who accepts the entire Bible as fully authoritative. If we were talking here only in theological terms, we who are evangelicals could level criticisms against American Protestantism and remain ourselves comfortably undisturbed, for we could attribute all faults to doctrinal liberalism. But when we speak of such matters as class divisions, racial discrimination, institutionalism, neglect of the poor and the inner city, and lack of social conscience and cultural impact, we are confronting problems that are just as present (and sometimes more so) in evangelical and fundamentalist churches as in the so-called liberal churches.

Proposals Heretical and Insufficiently Radical The church today is not without proposals for renewal, of course. But most of these suggestions are either heretical or insufficiently radical. They are heretical: They scrap the biblical gospel for something more "relevant." Or they are not radical enough: They try to hold on to too much of existing church tradition, organization and structure. Most programs for renewal from evangelical authors fall into the latter category, with some few notable exceptions.[2]

Many in evangelical churches know, of course, that Something Is Wrong. Some significant books by evangelicals—such as Robert Coleman's little classic, *The Master Plan of Evangelism* —have attempted to set forth New Testament principles of what the church should be and how it should evangelize. The problem is that almost none of these books goes far enough. The books on New Testament methods of evangelism, for instance, are good, but they attempt to graft some New Testament methods into ecclesiastical structures which are decidedly not New Testament in nature. In contrast, many of the books which deal specifically with the problems of structure all but forget the all-important biblical emphasis on proclamation and church extension; the living pulse of evangelistic proclamation is stopped by turning it into a third-person "kerygma." And often their suggestions about structure do not take seriously enough the New Testament concept of the church.

For a radical gospel (the biblical kind) we need a radical church (the biblical kind). For the ever-new wine we must continually have new wineskins.

In short, we need a cataclysm.

Something could be done. The institutionalism could be stripped away.

What would a denomination do that really wanted to become a church with New Testament dynamic? Let us suppose . . .

First, all church buildings are sold. The money is given (literally) to the poor. All congregations of more than two hundred members are divided in two. Store fronts, garages or small halls are rented as needed. Sunday school promotion and most publicity is dropped. Small group Bible studies meeting in private homes take the place of midweek prayer services.

Pastors take secular employment and cease to be paid by the church; they become, in effect, trained "laymen" instead of paid professionals. "Laymen" take the lead in all affairs of the church. There is no attempt to attract unbelievers to church services; these are primarily for believers, and perhaps are held at some time other than Sunday morning.

Evangelism takes on new dimensions. The church begins to take seriously its charge to preach the gospel to the poor and be an agent of the kingdom of God. It ceases to take economic potential into consideration in planning new churches. It begins to lose its enchantment with suburban materialism.

Et cetera.

What would happen to such a church? I suggest it would grow—and it might very well re-create the book of Acts.

This is the needed cataclysm, in general outline if not in specific detail. This cataclysm would bring the church close to the New Testament model and spirit. But it is an impossible cataclysm. No denomination in its right institutional mind will ever do such a thing, for perfectly good psychological and sociological (if not biblical) reasons.

Dietrich Bonhoeffer—to whom everyone seems to be in debt these days—wrote thirty years ago,

The Church is the Church only when it exists for others. To make a start, it should give away all its property to those in need. The clergy must live solely on the free-will offerings of their congregations, or possibly engage in some secular calling. The Church must share in the secular problems of ordinary human life, not dominating, but helping and serving. It must tell men of every calling what it means to live in Christ, to exist for others.[3]

This, in essence if not in detail, is the kind of cataclysm we need. But, unfortunately, it is an impossible one.

Or is it?

Is not God still saying, "I will do a new thing . . ."?

2
WORLD COME OF AGE?

The church at the end of the twentieth century should take a look at the kind of world we are living in.

When Dietrich Bonhoeffer wrote from his Nazi prison cell that the world had "come of age," he launched an idea that was to echo throughout the church world for decades. But what did he mean? Has the world really come of age? If so, what does this mean for the church and its mission and structure?

Bonhoeffer believed the world had come of age in the sense that the hypothesis of God is no longer considered necessary to account for man and his world. This is true, he said, not only in science and philosophy, but now even in religion itself.

Bonhoeffer noted, "Since Kant [God] has been relegated to a realm beyond the world of experience."[1] Bonhoeffer insisted that a realistic Christian apologetic must openly accept man's new godlessness and, in the midst of his own new scientific worldview, confront him with Christ. Said Bonhoeffer, "We should frankly recognize that the world, and people, have come of age."[2] "The world that has come of age is more godless, and perhaps for that very reason nearer to God, than the world before its coming of age."[3] His concern, he said, was "how to claim for Jesus Christ a world that has come of age."[4]

But was Bonhoeffer right? Has the world really come of age? What kind of world *is* ours?

It is a world secularized and urbanized, a "seculurban" world. Yet it is also a world where new superstitions rush in where old dogmas feared to tread; a world where city man can be just as isolated and insulated—and just as parochial—as his rural forebears. The secular city is becoming re-enchanted.

Secular man (with the possible exception of some "secular theologians") is facing a failure of nerve. What was heralded as man's adulthood, his secular confidence, is being termited by self-doubt.

To what age *has* man come? Where are we on the roadmap of world history?

Rather than having come of age, history has come full circle. It has returned in several key respects to the spirit of the first-century Roman world. And therefore this age to which we have come may be *the most strategic one for the effective proclamation of the biblical gospel.*

E. M. Blaiklock has observed, "Of all the centuries, the twentieth is most like the first: city-ridden, marred by tyranny, decadent, and wracked by those crises that man's abuse of man and of his native earth engenders."[5] This parallel between today's civilization and the first-century world has also been suggested by futurologists Herman Kahn and Anthony J. Wiener of the Hudson Institute. In their 1967 book *The Year 2000* they note that "there are some parallels between Roman times and ours" and suggest that "some of the prospects for the year 2000 are, in effect, a return to a sort of new Augustinian age."[6] Discussing current culture, they say that "something very much like our multi-fold trend occurred in Hellenistic Greece, the late Roman Republic, and the early Roman Empire."[7]

Kahn and Wiener's "multifold trend" is in the direction of "increasingly sensate, secular, pragmatic cultures; the accumulation and application of scientific and technological knowledge; the increasing tempo and institutionalization of change; and increasing education, urbanization, and affluence."[8]

This analysis is interesting when placed alongside Adolf Harnack's list of first-century conditions which particularly aided the growth of the Christian faith. Some of the parallels with today's conditions are striking, particularly when Harnack speaks of "the blending of different nationalities," "the comparative unity of language and ideas," "the practical and theoretical conviction of the essential unity of mankind," and, especially, "the rising vogue of a mystical philosophy of religion with a craving for some form of revelation and a thirst for miracle."[9]

Seven Signs of the Times A comparison of the cultural climate of the late twentieth century with that of the first-century Roman Empire yields several significant parallels.

1. *An essentially urban world with cities playing the major cultural role.* The urban flavor of the first century comes through clearly in the book of Acts and in Paul's writings. In contrast to most of the Middle Ages and the first 150 years of American history, "the Graeco-Roman world was a congeries of cities," according to historian Kenneth Latourette.[10] It was the world of Rome, Alexandria, Ephesus, Corinth, Colossae, Thessalonica, Sardis, Philadelphia, Smyrna, Laodicea, Ancyra, Antioch (capital of Syria and said to be the third city in the empire) and literally hundreds of other cities. Rome, the largest, had a first-century population of possibly one million, and the population of Alexandria has been estimated at 500,000. Many cities apparently had populations in excess of 100,000 (including slaves); we know the stadium at Ephesus could seat 25,000.[11]

Estimates vary for the first-century population of the total Roman Empire, but sixty million seems a reasonable figure. Of this total perhaps as many as ten million, or about 15%, lived in major cities of 100,000 or more. Considering the large number of smaller cities then in existence, perhaps nearly half the population lived in cities—a situation that later changed drastically.

The important fact, however, is not one of percentages but of influence. Regardless of the percentage actually urbanized (by today's standards), it is clear that urban life and culture played the predominant role in the first century. The city was the place to be; the book of Acts reflects this.

The fact of urbanization today—not only in America but worldwide—is too well-known to need elaboration. We say ours is an urban age, which it is, even though in actual fact only about 25% of the world population lives in metropolitan areas of more than 100,000.[12]

Thus one can trace an urban parallel between the Roman Empire and the world today—statistically, but especially culturally. For urbanization is more than a quantitative development. Harvey Cox notes, "Urbanization means a structure of common life in which diversity and the disintegration of tradition are paramount," in which "high mobility, economic concentration, and mass communication have drawn even rural villages into the web of urbanization."[13] Despite Cox's contention that this is a strictly twentieth-century phenomenon, the first-century parallel is significant.

2. *Unparalleled peace, stability and political unity.* "War is one of the constants of history," wrote the Durants in *The Lessons of History.* "In the last 3421 years of recorded history only 268 have seen no war."[14] Yet the Christian faith burst into the Roman world during a time of unusual peace. Caesar Augustus had stabilized the entire empire, bringing about "a time of peace unparalleled in history."[15]

At first glance today's world does not look very pacific. We think of Indochina, the Middle East, some areas of Africa; of political, economic and racial strife, and so on. Yet by contrast with the past, and considering today's lightning social revolutions, the era since 1945 has been remarkably peaceful. Despite local turbulence, the world today demonstrates a surprising overall stability. For many, a major world war seems less likely now than it did just ten years ago.

Certainly no worldwide political unity comparable to the Roman Empire's position in the Mediterranean world exists today. Yet the far-flung American military and economic presence, plus the caution induced by nuclear fear, plus the expanding web of technological advance, plus other factors, have produced what may be a "functional equivalent" of the Roman Empire and the Pax Romana. Even the United Nations, for all its ineffectiveness, has been a stabilizing influence.

3. *The worldwide spread of one predominant culture and language.* Greek culture predominated in the first-century Roman world. Throughout the Roman Empire, even in Italy, Greek was the common second language. Greek ideas were adopted or mimicked in nearly every province. Roman children were taught in Greek.

The parallel with American influence today (for good or ill) is striking. School children from Russia to China study English. The world goes to American movies and adopts American styles. America is still the world's primary exporter of technological and scientific innovation, even though Japan's influence has been growing in this area.

4. *International travel, communication and cultural interchange.* Roman roads (52,000 miles of them, according to one estimate[16]) are legendary; their safety and maintenance in the first century find parallel only in our day. Businessmen, government officials, military personnel and others traveled extensively and with ease throughout the empire. Knowledge and communication mushroomed, creating something like a first-century equivalent of our knowledge explosion. Harnack speaks of "the ubiquitous merchant and soldier—one may add, the ubiquitous professor."[17]

The situation is similar today, but now on a nearly worldwide scale. Never before has travel been so easy, so safe, so comparatively cheap or so extensive. Businessmen, students, educators, churchmen, tourists, athletes and government personnel travel constantly to almost all parts of the globe. Even China is beginning to open up. Worldwide travel has reached unparalleled levels. Cultural exchange—both official and unofficial—goes on apace, often unnoticed.

Then there is the world of modern mass communications—satellites, national and international publications (at newsstands in São Paulo, Brazil, one can often find *Time, L'Express, Stern* and other foreign magazines), the wire services, unprecedented book publishing and television. The dramatic demonstration of this system was the worldwide live TV coverage of the first manned moon landing in 1969.

In short, ours is the communications age. New ideas and events quickly become the possession of the world. The situation is unparalleled, but, on its own scale, the first century was remarkably similar.

5. *Pervasive social change, with a tendency toward a humanizing, universalist, "one world" outlook; a feeling that mankind is essentially one and shares a common destiny.* Any broad movement of men and ideas tends to unravel the fabric of tradition and produce social change. This was true in the days of the early church. Harnack cites Ulhorn's description of the first-century world: *Ancient life had by this time begun to break up; its solid foundations had begun to weaken. . . . The idea of universal humanity had disengaged itself from that of nationality. The Stoics had passed the word that all men were equal, and had spoken of brotherhood as well as the duties of man toward man. Hitherto despised, the lower classes had asserted their position. The treatment of slaves became milder. . . . Women, hitherto without any legal rights, received such in increasing numbers. Children were looked after. The distribution of grain . . . became a sort of poor-relief or welfare system, and we meet with a growing number of generous deeds, gifts, and endowments, which already exhibit a more humane spirit.*[18]

This description depicts not only the age of Paul but also, to a surprising degree, the contemporary world.

Zbigniew Brzezinski says in *Between Two Ages,* "We . . . have reached the stage in mankind's history where the passion for equality is a universal, self-conscious force. . . . The passion of equality is strong today because for the first time in human history inequality is no longer insulated by time and distance."[19] Scaled down to fit the first century, nearly the same could have been said of the Roman Empire. The passion for equality was not as great, but it was present and growing. And its essential presupposition, namely, that mankind is basically one, was a powerful molding force then as now.

6. *Widespread religious and philosophical ferment; the mixture and "relativization" of worldviews; the rise of new religions; a practical atheism and disbelief in the gods, coupled with an existential mysticism.* Here we have, theologically, the most characteristic first-century condition—and the most important one from the standpoint of the Christian faith. Latourette notes, "In this ethical, philosophical, and religious ferment is one of the chief reasons for Christianity's remarkable spread."[20] And it is here the parallel with today's world is the most impressive.

We may mention four more or less distinct first-century trends here. The first was a practical atheism resulting from a strong reaction against traditional religion and its gods. Popular writers ridiculed the gods of traditional mythology. "Thoughtful people reflected on the cruelties, adulteries, deceits, battles and lies attributed to the gods, and they were repelled."[21] By many, traditional religion was no longer taken seriously.

A similar development is taking place today. There is growing disenchantment with both ideology and traditional religion, whether this takes the form of rising scepticism about the truth of Marxism in communist countries, the abandonment of historic beliefs in Africa and the Orient, or reaction against institutionalized Christianity in the West. Ours is "the age of volatile belief" (Brzezinski), of "the end of ideology"

(Daniel Bell), of "relativized worldviews" (Harvey Cox). As Brzezinski notes,

In our time the established ideologies are coming under attack because their institutionalized character, which was once useful in mobilizing the relatively uneducated masses, has become an impediment to intellectual adaptation, while their concern with the external qualities of life is increasingly felt to ignore the inner, more spiritual dimension.

Compelling ideologies thus are giving way to compulsive ideas, . . . Yet there is still a felt need for a synthesis that can define the meaning and the historical thrust of our times.[22]

Second, this religious ferment was characterized by the rise of new, intensely emotional religions and the resurgence of some of the older oriental faiths. In the Roman Empire the cults of Cybele, Isis and Mithras (the last imported from Persia) were particularly popular, but there were many others. "By the first century A. D. the Graeco-Roman world was inundated with mystery cults of this sort," writes Michael Green, and "the enthusiasm engendered by these cults was great."[23]

This development also finds many present-day parallels—the resurgence of some Buddhist sects, the popularity in the West of various Indian gurus, the phenomenal spread of spiritism, in various forms, in Brazil, and the new religions of Japan, of which Soka Gakkai is the best known. These and similar movements have in common an intense emotional nature in which experience overshadows specific belief.[24]

A related parallel here is the popularity of astrology. Green cites "the rise and great popularity of the pseudo-science of astrology in the last century B. C."[25] The contemporary resurgence of astrology is well-known and has been recorded in the popular press.[26]

A third aspect of first-century religious ferment was the rise of an irrational mysticism and an emphasis on experience rather than reason. Notes Latourette, "The intellectuals were despairing of the ability of the unaided human mind to arrive at truth."[27] As we have already observed, Harnack mentions this as one of the "external conditions" of the first-century world.

The situation today looks like a replay of the first century. Both a contemporary conservative Protestant (Francis Schaeffer) and a secular political scientist (Zbigniew Brzezinski) have spoken of man's "escape from reason." *Experiencing* is the thing, whether through political radicalism, drugs, communal living, glossolalia or oriental mysticism; one has only to look at the mess we are in today, it is said, to see where rationalism leads. A return to romanticism has set in.[28]

A fourth trend indicating religious ferment was a general theological and ideological confusion and a quest for new directions. For the first century, this was largely the fruit of rising disbelief in the traditional gods. The popularization of Plato's philosophy and his attacks on the gods left thinkers of the day in a philosophical and theological vacuum. The traditional gods were dead. What was to replace them?

The modern parallel here is the theological confusion of the sixties with its various bizarre spin-offs and the contemporary movement putting in question the whole development of Western thought since Descartes and Kant and calling for a new biblical theology. Robert J. Blaikie's book *"Secular Christianity" and God Who Acts* and Francis Schaeffer's *The God Who Is There* are significant in this regard.[29]

7. *Moral degeneration.* I add this last parallel with some hesitation, since it has been so often cited and so frequently overworked. In connection with what has previously been said, however, it does seem a legitimate parallel between the contemporary world and the world of the early church. The progressive, inexorable, even predictable exploitation of sex and violence today, leading directly into homosexuality and sado-masochism, is probably unparalleled since Roman times.

Three Objections Where there are parallels there are also contrasts. Three differences between today and the first century may be considered.

First, our age stands at the end of twenty centuries of Christian history, whereas the first century was a pre-Christian age. Considering this, are the parallels we have drawn really valid?

While this difference is important, it does not disqualify the main point I am making in this chapter, for two reasons. One is that Judaism had spread rapidly throughout the Roman world during the four centuries prior to Pentecost, both as a religious faith and as a perspective on reality. During this time Judaism was an intensely missionary faith,[30] and we may suppose that its leavening influence was something parallel to the role of Christianity today and in past centuries.

The other qualifying factor is Christianity's remarkable self-renewing capacity. Many times at the very moment in history when the visible, institutional church was dying and funeral preparations were underway, the Christian faith was quietly being reborn in new movements and wineskins which only later became recognized. There is some evidence that this is happening today. Christianity may be, *at one and the same time,* one of the old, traditional religions being abandoned *and* one of the new, dynamic, emerging faiths. The so-called Jesus Revolution in the United States was one example of this.

A second difference is the totally new fact of computerized technology, the "technetronic revolution." Here there is no real first-century parallel. Yet there is something of a negative parallel. While computerized technology is a new fact, many react against it by turning to irrationalism and mysticism—a response which parallels the first-century reaction against contemporary philosophy and science.

The implications of the technological revolution for the Christian faith will be far-reaching and need to be studied thoroughly. Jacques Ellul's books, especially *The Technological Society* and *The Meaning of the City,* are particularly important here. I will have more to say later about the importance of the technological revolution for the church.

Finally, the Roman Empire was not really the whole world, but only a restricted part of it, whereas today we think in truly worldwide terms. But this is precisely the point I am making. We are seeing emerge a situation similar to that of the first-century Roman Empire, *but today on a worldwide scale*. Christianity was born into this Roman world "in the fullness of time" and turned it upside down. May not this happen again in our age—worldwide?

Sometimes we are shocked and dismayed by crime statistics and other indicators of moral decline or by other signs of the crisis of human culture. But rather than be dismayed, perhaps we should look at these indications in another light. For we as Christians know that the true church of Jesus Christ can never be in any real danger of extinction. Institutionalized religion may decline. Immorality may grow. But even through these things God may be preparing a new revolutionary outbreak of the gospel that will once again alter the course of human history. Christ came "in the fullness of time," when the stage was set. And God is setting the stage today for a great moving of his hand—perhaps the last great moving in the world's history.

There are encouraging signs—the Jesus Movement among North American youth, widespread new experiments in Christian communal living,[31] unprecedented evangelical publishing, fantastic Pentecostal growth in Latin America, revival in Indonesia and some parts of Africa, new openness to the gospel among Hindus in India, new and persuasive voices in evangelical theology. It may indeed be that the world is coming of age in the most profound sense—coming to recognize its utter need for a sure word from the living God.

The needed cataclysm in the institutional church still looks impossible. But maybe the overflowing new wine will find new wineskins.

Prophecies such as Joel 2:28-32 were not completely exhausted on the day of Pentecost. A fund of biblical prophecies remains stored up for our day, and not all of these prophecies speak negatively of judgment.[32] God will yet do a new thing!

And it shall come to pass afterward, that I will pour out my Spirit on all flesh; your sons and your daughters shall prophesy, your old men shall dream dreams, and your young men shall see visions. Even upon the menservants and the maidservants in those days, I will pour out my spirit. . . . And all who call upon the name of the LORD shall be delivered. (Joel 2:28-29, 32)

With the world coming full circle and conditions so strikingly similar to New Testament days, it is not unreasonable to hope for the emergence of a church with New Testament dynamic.

And a church with New Testament dynamic is one which preaches the gospel to the poor.

3
THE GOSPEL TO THE POOR

Jesus came preaching the gospel to the poor. The Old Testament repeatedly speaks of God's care for the poor, the fatherless, the widow, the oppressed. What does this biblical concern for the poor mean for the life of the church today?

There is loose in the contemporary Protestant church the idea that solid, self-supporting churches cannot be planted among the poor, at least not without heavy subsidies and leadership from richer churches. There is some truth to this—*if* we are talking about churches modeled after the traditional institutionalized pattern of expensive buildings and corporate-style organization. But if our concern is to plant New Testament churches, we had better take a second look at the New Testament gospel. And what it says about the poor.

An examination of biblical references to the poor convinces me that there is a special biblical concern for the poor, and that in general the church today is neglecting this concern—to its own hurt.[1] This concern is integrally related to the question of church structure, as we shall see.

Jesus certainly put no restrictions on the Great Commission; the good news is to be carried to every nation and class. And yet by both statement and example Jesus shows that the poor have a special place in the plan of God. And the entire Bible is remarkably consistent in sounding this theme.

The Poor in the Old Testament From the Mosaic covenant to the promises of the gospel, the Bible is continually pointing to the poor, the widow, the orphan, the stranger, the needy and the oppressed.

The Old Testament reveals several significant facts, surprising facts, about God's attitude toward the poor. We read that the Lord especially loves the poor and does not forget them. God's anointed one "delivers the needy when he calls, the poor and him who has no helper. He has pity on the weak and the needy, and saves the lives of the needy" (Ps. 72:12-13). The Lord "does not forget the cry of the afflicted" (Ps. 9:12). God has been "a stronghold to the poor, a stronghold to the needy in his distress" (Is. 25:4).

In the Old Testament social order the poor received an economic advantage. The people were commanded to loan freely to the poor, but not to charge interest (Deut. 15:7-11; Ex. 22:25). Part of the wheat and grape harvest was to be left ungathered for the benefit of the poor (Lev. 19:9-10; 23:22). Significantly, part of the purpose of the tithe was to provide relief for the poor (Deut. 14:29; 26:12-13).

The Old Testament emphasizes that God requires justice for the poor and will judge those who oppress them. God's words by the prophet Zechariah are representative: "Render true judgments, show kindness and mercy each to his brother, do not oppress the widow, the fatherless, the sojourner, or the poor" (Zech. 7:9-10; compare Lev. 19:15; Deut. 16:18-20; 24:14-22; Prov. 31:9; Amos 2:6-7).

Finally, the Old Testament teaches that God's people bear a special ethical responsibility for the poor. Remembrance of their slavery in Egypt was to motivate the Israelites to show mercy to the oppressed (Deut. 24:17-22). The faithfulness of God's people was continually measured by their treatment of the poor.

All these teachings about the poor are part of God's Word. Although they are tied to specific historical contexts, the ethical message shines through and forms the background of Jesus' own attitude and teachings. The teaching is clear, and both consistent and persistent: Of all peoples and classes, God especially has compassion on the poor, and his acts in history confirm this.

It is relevant here to ask *why* God is thus concerned for the poor. What is there within the nature of God which requires such special attention? To answer this fully we would have to consider in detail the biblical concept of *justice.* In the Old Testament God's concern with the poor consistently appears within the context of the justice of God and the working of justice among God's people. Thus, biblically, words such as *the poor, the needy, the oppressed, the sojourner* typically have moral content, relating to God's requirement for justice.

This is not easily comprehended in today's world because *the poor* does not have such a moral content for us. It has a purely descriptive sense; one might say that for us it is a purely secular word. But what we must see is that poverty itself is of ethical significance—*the poor* is a moral category. In God's world there is no human condition which escapes moral significance, and the poor, and the treatment they receive, are strong indicators of the faithfulness of God's people.

Jesus and the Poor But what of Jesus and the poor? Did Jesus play down the Old Testament emphasis, or did he affirm it? Several facts about Jesus' attitude toward the poor can be discerned in the Gospels.

1. *Jesus made the preaching of the gospel to the poor a validation of his own ministry.* He said, "The Spirit of the Lord is upon me, because he has anointed me to preach good news to the poor" (Lk. 4:18-21). And he cited Isaiah 61 to show by what marks his gospel could be known. He plainly said that it was his *practice* and *conscious intent* to preach his gospel especially to the poor. (Compare Mt. 11:1-6.)

2. *Jesus believed the poor were more ready and able to understand*

and accept his gospel. An amazing thing, and how different from common attitudes in the church today! On one occasion Jesus prayed, "I thank thee, Father, Lord of heaven and earth, that thou hast hidden these things from the wise and understanding and revealed them to babes; yea, Father, for such was thy gracious will" (Mt. 11:25-26). Here Jesus indicated that "the wise and understanding"—the sophisticated, the educated, those of higher social status—find the gospel difficult to accept, a stumbling block, while "babes"—those of little sophistication and understanding—are quick to grasp the meaning of, and accept, the good news. Clearly the poor are in the latter category. "While he was Lord of the whole world, he preferred *children and ignorant persons to the wise,*" said John Calvin.[2]

3. *Jesus specifically directed the gospel call to the poor.* He said, "Come to me, all who labor and are heavy laden, and I will give you rest" (Mt. 11:28). Despite the almost universal tendency to spiritualize these words, by the context it seems clear that Jesus was speaking, in the first place, literally. Jesus' call was pre-eminently to the poor—those who, of all people, are the most wearied and burdened, not only spiritually but also from long hours of physical labor and the various oppressions known only to the poor. To these—not exclusively, but pre-eminently—Jesus was speaking. Walter Rauschenbusch was right in saying, "The fundamental sympathies of Jesus were with the poor and oppressed."[3]

4. *On several occasions Jesus recommended showing partiality to the poor.* (See, for example, Mt. 19:21; Lk. 12:33; 14:12-14.) In this he was in complete harmony with the spirit of God's revelation in the Old Testament.

In short, Jesus Christ, the Son of God, demonstrated the same attitude toward the poor that God revealed in the Old Testament. Though the Savior of all men, he looked with special compassion upon the poor. He purposely took the gospel to the poor, and specifically called attention to what he was doing.

This is, in summary, the biblical evidence. That there *is* biblical evidence for God's particular concern for the poor is obvious if one takes the trouble to look for it.

The Gospel to the Poor Today What do the biblical teachings about the poor mean for our churches today? The implications are clear and urgent.

1. *Like her Master, the church must place special emphasis on the poor.* A biblical theology for today must reflect the biblical concern for the poor. A church that seeks to be New Testament in spirit and practice will need to think through the implications of this biblical emphasis.

This truth must be urgently affirmed today because contemporary Protestantism is, in general, neglecting the lower classes. Bruce Kendrick in his book on the East Harlem Protestant Parish has described the contemporary neglect of the poor in these terms: "Instead of seeking the lost sheep—whether black or white or speckled—[Protestants] sought out those who thought as they thought, and dressed as they dressed, and talked as they talked." Instead of seeking the poor, "the Protestant church was cutting itself off from them and neglecting the fact that the sign of the Kingdom is that the poor have the Gospel preached to them."[4] "By leaving the ghetto behind," writes David McKenna, "the church has implied that its mission is meaningless to the poor, the hopeless, and the wretched—except when an ocean separates the church from the ghetto."[5]

Even if somewhat exaggerated, these criticisms are uncomfortably close to the truth. Not that Protestant denominations do not have poor or working-class people in them; of course, many of them do. The point is that there is an almost total lack of awareness of the church's responsibility to *seek out* the poor, to plan for church growth among the poor, rather than to treat them primarily as a social problem to be discussed and analyzed. "I was hungry, and you gave me a press release."

In America, the gospel to the poor implies an especial Christian responsibility for the inner city, for the inner city is the particular kingdom of the poor. "The life of the inner city is a mixture of many things; nevertheless, its dominant note is poverty," observes Gibson Winter.[6]

We must recognize, however, that the poor are not always confined to the inner city. There are poor suburbs as well as middle-class and upper-class ones. Also, urbanization patterns vary from country to country, and the poor are not always to be found in the central city. Often they are found in the outer ring of the city, as in São Paulo, Brazil. But wherever the poor are found, there is the focus of Christian responsibility.

The basic issue is not a question of geography. Christian faithfulness is not necessarily measured by where one lives, although in some cases it may be. The basic issue is Christian responsibility for the poor. If Christians move from a particular area, they must ask themselves what this move means for their responsibility toward the poor. What are their motives for moving? Where can they best build the church? Are they leaving the poor behind? If so, whose responsibility are these poor? Does the move represent greater or less obedience to the gospel? Facing such hard questions in the light of the Scriptures may be the only way to break the pattern of leaving the poor spiritually disinherited.

2. *The priority among the poor is evangelism.* Our concern must be, in the first instance, with the central truth of the gospel message: reconciliation between God and man through the blood of Jesus Christ.

It is Jesus himself who sets this priority: "The Spirit of the Lord is upon me, because he has anointed me *to preach good news to the poor*" (Lk. 4:18). "The blind receive their sight and the lame walk, lepers are cleansed and the deaf hear, and the dead are raised up, and the poor have *good news preached* to them" (Mt. 11:5).

In all our concern for the poor, we are in critical danger of neglecting or withholding the most important help we can give: the message of the gospel itself. Nothing we can do for the poor is more relevant than evangelism. As Ernest Campbell has said in his *Christian Manifesto*, "A church so busily at work correcting the massive injustices of society that it cannot or will not make the effort to win men and women to an allegiance to Jesus Christ will soon become sterile and unable to produce after its kind."[7] Nor will its kind be worth producing after.

Today many evangelicals are a little embarrassed, or so it seems, to talk of evangelizing the poor because of past excesses and a one-sided preoccupation with "souls." This is understandable, but no excuse for abandoning the proclamation of the good news. The gospel must be the primary emphasis—not because it is the way to attack social problems but because "the wages of sin is death, but the free gift of God is eternal life" (Rom. 6:23).

Are we more concerned, perchance, with poverty than with the poor? More concerned about a program than about people? Is our first interest to solve a social problem or to meet personal need? We may say that the former accomplishes the latter, but that is not necessarily so. The problem of poverty may one day be solved, but the poor—or formerly poor—still be left without the gospel.

Obviously, Christ-centered evangelism will not compartmentalize. It will not divide up people into "soul" and "body," caring for the one and condemning those who care for the other. Leighton Ford has written, "Like our Lord, who healed the sick and fed the hungry, we must see men as whole men, not as disembodied souls to be prepackaged for heaven."[8] Thus Christ-centered evangelism will care for people—people in sin, people lost and oppressed, laboring and heavy laden people, hungry for real food and for real fellowship. It will walk as Christ walked, but it will always tell why Christ died. It will proclaim Jesus as human example, but supremely as risen Lord.

There is another fact that suggests the priority of evangelism: The poor are, in general, more receptive to the gospel. Jesus was right!

Ernst Troeltsch observed some sixty years ago, "The really creative, church-forming religious movements are the work of the lower strata. . . . Need upon the one hand and the absence of an all-relativizing culture of reflection on the other hand are at home only in these strata."[9] Historically this has been true: Church growth has been most rapid among the poor. Sociologically speaking, the roots of Christianity have most often been among the masses. Troeltsch also wrote, "The Early Church sought and won her new adherents chiefly among the lower classes in the cities, . . . members of the well-to-do, educated upper classes only began to enter the Church in the second century, and then only very gradually."[10] Tertullian could say in the second century, "The uneducated are always a majority with us." John Wesley said in 1771, "Every where we find the labouring part of mankind the readiest to receive the Gospel."[11]

Recent studies by the McGavran Church Growth school have borne out the same pattern. One good example is the case of Adoniram Judson, famous missionary to Burma. Judson sought out the higher class Burmese as the people to evangelize. But along the way he took in a poor member of the despised and uneducated Karen tribe. This man, Ko Tha Byu, became a thorough Christian and began carrying the gospel to his own people, while Judson worked with the social elite. What happened? Great numbers of Karens turned to Christ, while relatively little fruit was seen by Judson.[12] Obviously other factors were also at work here, but a characteristic pattern appears: rapid growth of the faith among the poor.

Many similar examples come out of the history of Christian missions in the last two centuries, particularly in India. Donald McGavran gives the following account in *Understanding Church Growth:*

In 1840 the American Baptists started a mission at Nellore on the eastern coast of India. For twenty-five years they labored among the upper castes, winning less than a hundred converts.

In 1865 John Clough and his wife came out as new missionaries. As they learned the language and studied the Bible to see what God would have them do, each independently came to the conclusion that, on the basis of 1 Corinthians 1:26-28, the policy followed rigorously by the elder missionaries of seeking to win only the upper castes was displeasing to God. The Madigas (Untouchables), known to be responsive to the Christian message, had been bypassed lest their baptism make it still more difficult for caste Hindus to become Christians. The Cloughs moved from Nellore, opened the station of Ongole, and began baptizing some remarkably earnest and spiritual Madiga leaders. By 1869, hundreds were being added to the Lord.[13]

In his significant study of church growth in Brazil, William R. Read notes a similar pattern, especially among Pentecostals: "People in the lower strata of Brazilian society generally accept the Christian message more readily than the more privileged who are found in the upper classes." And this is a predominantly urban pattern: "The Pentecostals have been active and successful in the highly populated urban centers to which flow large numbers of migrating peoples from rural districts."[14] My own experience in Brazil bears this out.

It is no secret that many of today's great denominations—hardly to be classed as poor today—had their beginning as Christward movements among the lower classes. The period of phenomenal growth came during those years when the gospel was preached to the poor.

This fact of rapid church growth among the poorer classes says something about strategy and stewardship. As McGavran points out, planting the gospel seed where it is most likely to grow is faithful stewardship of the gospel message. I am convinced that Jesus commands us to preach the gospel to the poor not only because their need is most acute but also precisely because they are most ready to accept.

In short, both concern for personal conversion and considerations of church growth strategy say: The first priority among the poor is evangelism.

3. *Christian responsibility toward the poor does not end with evangelism.* Why? Because biblically it cannot. Because loving involvement with persons, once begun, cannot simply be turned off. Parents who love their children do not neglect their needs. They feed and clothe them—not because they are unconcerned about their souls but because in practice love is not greatly concerned with analytical distinctions between soul and body.

Therefore—since Christian responsibility toward the poor must be an expression of love—we cannot make rigid prescriptions about what exactly is Christian responsibility to the poor, beyond evangelism. Love will identify and meet the need in each specific context, if not walled in by unbiblical traditions that asphyxiate love.

We do have the Bible to guide us. It is clear from both Old and New Testament teachings, for example, that God expects his people to see that the poor among them are cared for. Can we say with David, "I have not seen the righteous forsaken or his children begging bread" (Ps. 37:25)? If not, we may question whether our church is meeting its biblical responsibility to the poor.

4. *The church needs the poor.* In fact, to maintain its spiritual dynamic it needs the poor much more than it needs the rich or the middle class.

Starting with Ernst Troeltsch, various students of the church as social phenomenon have observed how religious movements are born among the poor and then with succeeding generations rise on the socioeconomic ladder, leaving the poor behind, disinherited. H. Richard Niebuhr's *Social Sources of Denominationalism* (published in 1929) is still very relevant at this point. Said Niebuhr, "The churches of the poor all become middle-class churches sooner or later." Niebuhr documented the following now-familiar pattern:

One phase of the history of denominationalism reveals itself as the story of the religiously neglected poor, who fashion a new type of Christianity which corresponds to their distinctive needs, who rise in the economic scale under the influence of religious discipline, and who in the midst of a freshly acquired cultural respectability, neglect the new poor succeeding them on the lower plane. This pattern recurs with remarkable regularity in the history of Christianity.[15]

The question is, Is this pattern biblical? And is it inevitable, predestined? Clearly it is not biblical—not Christian—to neglect the poor, even though it is a common pattern. And if not biblical, neither is it inevitable. The church needs the poor. The churches of the middle class need the lower classes. If they would avoid spiritual and social hardening of the arteries, churches must be growing among the poor.

Every denomination needs a continuing infusion of hundreds of new members from among the poor—men and women saved right out of the crisis of their poverty. This would keep us shook up and spiritually alive. It would keep our churches from being captured by any one class or political philosophy, and thus from being compromised. Our radical differences in the world would unite us in Christ. Fellowship in the church would demand miracle: It would be the fellowship, literally, of the Holy Spirit. Impossible? It happened in the first century A.D.

The pattern of the flesh is for our churches to grow up into "respectability," leaving the poor behind. The pattern of the Spirit is for the church to grow up into Christ, as we read in Ephesians 4.

It is not surprising that Christians do, with time, tend to prosper materially. Increased faithfulness at work, more careful stewardship of money, a new concern for education, and similar factors, do bring economic and social advancement. Christian faithfulness generally brings material blessings.

The problem is not that Christians prosper; it is that in prospering they tend to turn their backs on the poor and adopt the social attitudes of their newly acquired status. Consciousness of the gospel's special call to the poor is either forgotten or spiritualized.

According to the Bible, the pattern should be different. In prospering materially, Christians should make special effort to spread the gospel among the poor. They now have the resources to do this! Pastors and Christian leaders should continually point to this biblical responsibility and help Christians fulfill it. This is necessary not only for the sake of the poor but also for the spiritual health of those who are *not* poor.

The church needs the poor. As her members naturally prosper materially "under the influence of religious discipline"—a legitimate fruit, if not a guaranteed result, of the gospel—she must deliberately, self-consciously, preach the gospel to the poor. The church needs constantly the spiritual dynamism, spontaneity, honesty and radical dedication that is found pre-eminently among the poor who have heeded the call of Christ. The way to permanent renewal and consistent growth may lie precisely here: in effective evangelism among the masses. A healthy emphasis on the gospel to the poor may be the surest antidote to institutionalism and irrelevant structures.

The Practice of the Principles What does all this mean in practice? How can churches today meet their responsibility to the poor?

The first step is *awareness* of this responsibility (almost totally lacking today) and *commitment* to do something about it. What I have said here is intended to bring about a step in that direction.

Beyond this, we should look for a biblical approach. This means that we do not automatically assume the necessity of an elaborate building- or organization-centered program. The approach should be people-centered—through personal witness, informal contacts, person-to-person (rather than primarily mass) communication and small Bible study groups in homes or other places. The first priority should be to win a nucleus of solid converts, then to use this primary cell to move out both in evangelism and social ministry to reach the larger community. Often the poor themselves, once solidly converted, can do more for Christ in their own communities than can imported, highly trained and well-funded specialists, primarily because they see the problems from the inside and feel their weight. They live them.

The need, therefore, is not for expensive, large-scale programs to carry the gospel to the poor.[16] The need is for ordinary committed Christians with the vision and dedication to work among the poor, to spend time with them, to live among them in some cases, to form, quietly and without fanfare, dynamic cells of Christian witness which multiply to transform the community for Christ.[17]

Such an approach automatically answers most questions about finances. A ministry among the poor is not expensive if based on biblical principles. Nothing can be clearer from the New Testament itself and from early church history. The initial "missionaries" may be supported by a local church or group of Christian families, or they may be self-supporting. But once a nucleus of converts has been formed, its own tithe will be sufficient to carry on the work. The expense is not monetary; it is, rather, the cost of discipleship.

This is not, of course, to rule out entirely the possibility of major church-sponsored programs of relief or social action among the poor. These may be helpful, but are strictly secondary forms of Christian ministry, and no substitute for evangelism among the poor on a more personal basis.

But is the ideal possible, given the contemporary situation? Can a middle-class church (for example) convincingly preach the gospel to the poor? If not, the ever-new wine of the gospel will burst the old wineskins and once again create new ones. The rich churches will be left to die, becoming Laodicean (Rev. 3:17), and the true church will once again spring up among the poor. There are some signs already that this is precisely what is beginning to happen in some areas.

In Brazil and other places the poor are responding to the good news. But in my mind's ear I hear someone "back home" objecting, "Yes, but that's on the mission field!" Indeed it is—in this case, São Paulo, Brazil, a sophisticated and growing city of over six million people. But today the whole world is a mission field—a mission field of cities. The urban poor have the same needs and the same hunger for Christ whether in São Paulo, Tokyo or Chicago. We think that in America the response would not be the same if the gospel were preached to the poor. But then, how do we know? We aren't there. We haven't tried.

There must be a new preaching of the gospel to the poor in our day. The biblical gospel demands it. What we should hope and pray for, what we should expect, is not merely a host of individual churches which are growing and dynamic. Our hope should be to touch off revolutionary spiritual movements that "get out of (our) control," but are controlled by the Holy Spirit. It has happened before; it is happening right now in some places; it can happen again.

We must have nothing short of revolution—a spiritual revolution on a worldwide scale, as occurred nineteen centuries ago. Both the Bible and church history point the same way: Preach the gospel to the poor.

But, again, *can* the gospel be preached to the poor today? Are contemporary churches in a condition to make such proclamation? The fact is that the greater part of contemporary Protestantism is caught in a stifling web of institutionalism.

The wineskins have grown rigid. It is not enough, therefore, merely to call for change or to proclaim the need for proclamation. The whole problem of wineskins—the *structure* of the church—must be dealt with.

The Poor and the Problem of Wineskins So the urgency to preach the gospel to the poor brings us right to the question of the church and the problem of wineskins. The gospel to the poor and the concept of the church are inseparably linked. Failure to minister to the poor testifies to more than unfulfilled responsibility; it witnesses to a distorted view of the church.

Church history illustrates this. As I have already commented, renewal in the church has usually meant the church's rebirth among the poor, the masses, the alienated. And with such resurgence has usually come the recovery of such essential New Testament emphases as community, purity, discipleship, the priesthood of believers and the gifts of the Spirit.

The Protestant Reformation provides the most striking case in point. As Niebuhr notes, "The failure of the Reformation to meet the religious needs of peasants and other disfranchised groups is a chapter writ large in history. With all its native religious fervor it remained the religion of the middle class and the nobility."[18] The Reformation trumpet call of salvation by faith wakened the hope of deliverance among the oppressed masses, but the second blast called forth the troops against those who were prepared to take the gospel call of "liberty to the oppressed" too literally. To an unfortunately large degree, the poor were betrayed by much of the Reformation.

Why? Doubtless the reasons are complex, involving many social, political and economic, as well as theological, factors. The significant thing for our discussion in this book is that the mainline Reformation was very largely limited to the question of personal salvation (soteriology); it hardly touched, in any practical way, the doctrine of the church (ecclesiology), although it brought a number of structural modifications. As Hendrick Hart suggests, "Even though the leaders of the Protestant Reformation sincerely intended to break with the traditional Roman Catholic conception of the church, nevertheless the tradition arising from the Reformation did not succeed in making that break."[19]

The presbyterian and congregational systems arising from the Reformation brought some practical improvements, but both systems rested on many an untested Roman Catholic assumption about the essential nature of the church. This is evident particularly in the doctrine of spiritual gifts and the general concept of ministry, where the Roman Catholic clergy-laity dichotomy was largely carried over.[20] The result is that modern Protestant churches—whether presbyterian, congregational or episcopal in form—are more impressive for their similarity than for their differences. Regardless of the label, much Protestant ecclesiology is based more on tradition than on Scripture.

The result of the mainline Reformation's neglect of the poor and of the doctrine of the church was the so-called Radical Reformation, and principally the Anabaptist Movement. According to Roland Bainton, Anabaptism was "the result of an effort to carry through more consistently the program of the restoration of primitive Christianity. . . . Much more drastically than any of their contemporaries [the Anabaptists] searched the Scriptures in order to recover the pattern of the early church."[21]

Anabaptism, as well as such related movements as Quakerism, "the Anglo-Saxon parallel to Anabaptism"[22] a century later, was largely a movement of the peasants and the poorer classes. In their radical simplicity, such groups sought to carry through the Reformation impulse to the practical level of the daily life and witness of the Christian community. Theologically, this involved an extension of the Reformation to ecclesiology and to church structure.

The result for the Anabaptists, of course, was persecution and near extermination. The best Anabaptist leaders were soon eliminated "by fire, water, and sword," often at the hands of the mainline Reformers or their followers.[23] But a remnant survived. Later such groups as the Mennonites and the Hutterites, through much suffering and persecution, carried on the same ideals.

It is beside the point that the Anabaptists, Mennonites, Quakers and similar groups, under pressure of persecution, went to some extremes. The significant thing is that these movements of "the gospel to the poor" sought to restore a more biblical understanding and practice of the church. And church history since the Reformation shows that it is precisely these groups (or the re-evaluation of them) which have sparked much of the contemporary impulse to re-examine the doctrine and structure of the church.

The need today is certainly not to attempt to mimic the radical reformers or to try now to carry through their program of reform.[24] The need is rather to see the importance of the New Testament understanding of the church for our day, to insist that "salvation by faith" must be connected to true Christian community and real discipleship. In the Reformation age that idea was too radical to be tolerated. Today it is not. Today when new things are happening and fresh winds are blowing, the problem of wineskins needs examination by those who would take seriously Jesus Christ's announcement that he came to preach the gospel to the poor.

It is to this problem that we now turn our attention, first looking critically at some old wineskins and then suggesting the way to some new ones.

PART 2: A NEW LOOK AT OLD WINESKINS

4

CHURCHES, TEMPLES AND TABERNACLES

Let us go back to the Old Testament for a moment.

We can learn a lot from Moses. The Mosaic covenant and the forty years in the wilderness not only formed the Hebrew faith; they also teach us much about the nature of the community of God's people—about the church.

The three central elements in the Mosaic covenant were sacrifice, priesthood and tabernacle. These together, as part of and coupled with the Mosaic law, constituted the revealed basis for the covenant relationship between God and his chosen people. They constituted the approved way to God, atonement, God dwelling with his people in covenant fidelity.

The amazing teaching of the New Testament, especially in the book of Hebrews, is that Jesus Christ is the fulfillment of sacrifice, priesthood and tabernacle. Jesus Christ is our great high priest; therefore we have need of no earthly priest (Heb. 4:14; 8:1). The priesthood has passed away, or rather, has been expanded, to include all believers (1 Pet. 2:9; Rev. 1:6).

So also Jesus Christ is the true and perfect sacrifice, offered once for all, so that no further sacrifice is either necessary or possible (Heb. 7:27; 9:14, 25-28; 1 Pet. 3:18). The sacrificial system has become completely superfluous because all that was prefigured in the Mosaic covenant was fulfilled in the death of Christ. There is no more sacrifice, except as the church presents herself as a "living sacrifice" (Rom. 12:1-2).

It is also true, but much less emphasized, that Jesus Christ is the fulfillment of the tabernacle (Heb. 8—9). "For Christ has entered, not into a sanctuary made with hands, a copy of the true one, but into heaven itself, now to appear in the presence of God on our behalf" (Heb. 9:24). Thus the need for an earthly tabernacle has passed away. "The Word became flesh and dwelt [literally, tabernacled] among us" (Jn. 1:14; compare Jn. 1:17). Jesus identified his body with the temple (Jn. 2:19-21).[1] He is Emmanuel, "God with us" (Mt. 1:23).

Christ's body is, in one sense, "the true tabernacle." Thus the community of believers, the "body of Christ," is also part of the true tabernacle. For the church is "God's house" (Heb. 3:6; 1 Tim. 3:15), a "holy temple" (Eph. 2:21; 2 Cor. 6:16), a "dwelling place of God in the Spirit" (Eph. 2:22).

Sacrifice, priesthood, tabernacle—all instituted through Moses in the Old Testament. Theologically, all passed away with the coming of Christ and the birth of the church. Historically, all passed away with the destruction of Jerusalem in A.D. 70. They had become irrelevant, anachronistic.

And so the church was born without priesthood, sacrifice or tabernacle because the church and Christ together were all three. The church faithfully embodied this truth for more than a century, and overran the Roman Empire.

The great temptation of the organized church has been to reinstate these three elements among God's people: to turn community into an institution. Historically, the church has at times succumbed. Returning to the spirit of the Old Testament, she has set up a professional priesthood, turned the Eucharist into a new sacrificial system and built great cathedrals. When this happens, a return to faithfulness must mean a return—in both soteriology and ecclesiology—to the profound simplicity of the New Testament. Usually, however, reformation in doctrine has not been accompanied by sufficiently radical reform in church structure.

The Importance of the Tabernacle The significance of the tabernacle must be singled out for special attention here—partly because it usually is not but primarily because it has significance for the church, for ecclesiology. Why should God be represented by a physical structure? Why a tent?

In the Mosaic covenant the tabernacle was the symbol of God's presence. "Let them make me a sanctuary, that I may dwell in their midst" (Ex. 25:8). The central idea was God's *habitation* with his people. God could not actually dwell in the hearts of his people because of their sin and rebelliousness; his habitation had to be symbolic. So God ordered the tabernacle built and laid it out to Moses in extravagant detail. It was to be made according to the blueprint revealed on the mount (Ex. 26:30; Acts 7:44; Heb. 8:5).

But for the church the tabernacle is fulfilled in the body of Christ, as we have seen. So the necessity of a physical tabernacle has passed away. Why? Because now God dwells with his people in the hearts and bodies of the believing community, through the inhabiting of the Holy Spirit. The Holy Spirit "dwells with you, and will be in you" (Jn. 14:17), Jesus said. If one loves and obeys Jesus, the Father and Son "will come to him and make our home with him" (Jn. 14:23). "I will come in and eat with him, and he with me" (Rev. 3:20).

Clearly, the central idea of the tabernacle is God's habitation, but in the New Testament God dwells within the hearts of his people, not just symbolically among the people. The veil has been torn in two; the stony heart transplanted with one of flesh. So the church is "a dwelling place of God in [or through] the Spirit" (Eph. 2:22).

There will also be an eternal, eschatological fulfillment of the idea of God's habitation. For when John sees the holy city descending from God, the first words he hears from the throne are, "Behold, the tabernacle of God is with men" (Rev. 21:3, AV; compare Ezek. 37:27-28). This is the meaning of the holy city: God's habitation eternally, spiritually, really and perfectly, with his people. Therefore naturally there is "no temple in the city, for its temple is the Lord God the Almighty and the Lamb" (Rev. 21:22). And has this not ever been God's design: a city without temples because God himself is its temple? Here all limitations of time and space have evaporated. God and man are in perfect communion. Eternally, there exists the fellowship, the *koinonia*, of the Holy Spirit.

So we see a threefold progression. First, God symbolically dwelling *among* his people in a physical structure called a tabernacle. Second, God actually dwelling *within the hearts* of his people through the Holy Spirit. Third, God dwelling *eternally* with his people, *in perfect spiritual communion,* in the age to come. The first reality points to the second, and the second to the third.

Tabernacle or Temple? But in going from Moses to Christ, we jump over twelve hundred years of the history of God's people —the age of the temple. With the reign of David and Solomon the tabernacle was replaced by the temple. Are tabernacle and temple identical in meaning? Or do they suggest different aspects of God's plan for the church?

Analyzing the Old Testament account, we can see a distinct difference between the tabernacle and the temple.

I marvel every time I read of the construction of the ark and the tabernacle in the Old Testament. This was the pattern of the ark of the covenant:

Make an ark of acacia wood; two cubits and a half shall be its length, a cubit and a half its breadth, and a cubit and a half its height. And you shall overlay it with pure gold, . . . And you shall cast four rings of gold for it and put them on its four feet, . . . And you shall put the poles into the rings on the sides of the ark, to carry the ark by them." (Ex. 25:10-14)

On top of this chest went the mercy seat, a magnificent golden cover with two cherubim, their wings stretched over the ark.

Consider this beautiful and costly creation, symbol of the

presence of the Almighty God, Creator of the universe—but with two poles sticking out the ends for carrying it! A marred symbol? No, a perfect symbol—symbol not only of a holy God, but also of a mobile God! God has not been captured there in the tent. Some day, maybe tomorrow, things are going to change. The cloud will start to move. The ark will be carried on. Yahweh is free to be unpredictable. He is always true to himself, but not necessarily to man's preconceptions. He will do a new thing.

The tabernacle is the symbol of God's presence with his people, and as such it is, supremely, a mobile symbol. Everything is made to be easily dismounted and carried. And this is not Moses' idea; it is according to the pattern revealed on the mountain, as Scripture emphasizes repeatedly. If the tabernacle represents God's presence, it certainly represents the dynamic nature of God and the mobility of God's people.

But, it may be objected, this is pressing the meaning too far. Naturally, the tabernacle had to be movable, for God's people were on a journey; its mobility has no further significance. But this is precisely the point! *God* initiated the journey; *he* required it to last forty years; *he* created a pilgrim people. This was Israel's great object lesson about the nature of their God. Before settling down in the promised land, they must learn what kind of God they serve. He is not a God to be confined to a land or a city or a temple; he is beyond all these. The only way to truly learn this is as a pilgrim people, and the tabernacle reflects this.

One of the most beautiful and significant passages in the Old Testament graphically pictures this mobility:

Whenever the cloud lifted from the tent, the Israelites struck camp, and at the place where the cloud settled, there they pitched their camp. At the command of the LORD they struck camp, and at the command of the LORD they encamped again, and continued in camp as long as the cloud rested over the Tabernacle. When the cloud stayed long over the Tabernacle, the Israelites remained in attendance on the LORD and did not move on; and it was the same when the cloud continued over the Tabernacle only a few days: at the command of the LORD *they remained in camp, and at the command of the* LORD *they struck camp. There were also times when the cloud continued only from evening till morning, and in the morning, when the cloud lifted, they moved on. Whether by day or by night, they moved as soon as the cloud lifted. Whether it was for a day or two, for a month or a year, whenever the cloud stayed long over the Tabernacle, the Israelites remained where they were and did not move on; they did so only when the cloud lifted. At the command of the* LORD *they encamped, and at his command they struck camp. At the* LORD*'s command given through Moses, they remained in attendance on the* LORD. *(Num. 9:17-23,* NEB*)*

So it was with the tabernacle. But the temple was different. It was stationary—permanent—and its meaning differs accordingly.

The tabernacle was God's idea; it was his design. He commanded it. But what of the temple? God sent word to King David,

Would you build me a house to dwell in? I have not dwelt in a house since the day I brought up the people of Israel from Egypt to this day, but I have been moving about in a tent for my dwelling. In all places where I have moved with all the people of Israel, did I speak a word with any of the judges of Israel, whom I commanded to shepherd my people Israel, saying, "Why have you not built me a house of cedar?" (2 Sam. 7:5-7)

King David was rich, prosperous and at peace. He said to Nathan the prophet, "See now, I dwell in a house of cedar, but the ark of God dwells in a tent" (2 Sam. 7:2). If the king has a royal house, why not God, too? Is it not logical? The recognition of proper priorities?

Thus the temple was David's idea, not God's. Further, David was king, and the monarchy was not God's idea either (1 Sam. 8:4-9). We may wonder whether there would ever have been a temple had there not been a king. But in both cases God accommodated his plan to man's desires, for his own purposes.

God allowed the temple to be built, but not by David. David made preparations and Solomon did the building. In contrast to the tabernacle, the blueprint did not come from Mount Sinai. God was not the architect.

While Solomon was building the temple, a word came from God: "Concerning this house which you [note *you*, not *I*] are building, if you will walk in my statutes and obey my ordinances and keep all my commandments and walk in them, then I will establish my word with you, which I spoke to David your father. And I will dwell among the children of Israel, and will not forsake my people Israel" (1 Kings 6:12-13). Although the temple is not God's idea, he honors Solomon's good intentions, even his creativity. He will dwell in the house; he will continue the covenant—*provided* Solomon and the people are faithful.[2]

Such was the beginning of the temple. Later the people disobeyed God and the temple was destroyed. The chosen people were carried into captivity. They thought God was safely within the temple and among the priests, but suddenly he came at them from outside, through the voice of the prophet and the thunder of foreign kings.

The conclusion from all this is clear: The truer sign of the presence of God in his earthly church is the tabernacle, and only secondarily the temple. The tabernacle is the truer symbol, for it more accurately shows how God acts in history.

A certain legitimacy does belong to the Old Testament temple, but this is essentially typological and eschatological, based on the Davidic kingdom as the type of Christ's eternal kingdom.[3] The typology comes through clearly in the Psalms, where David is the king, Jerusalem is the holy city and the temple is God's holy dwelling. But the primary significance is eschatological; in actual fact, David sins, the monarchy degenerates, the holy city is full of blood and the temple worship finally falls into a dead institutionalism.

This typical, eschatological interpretation is borne out further by what the prophets have to say about the temple. They frequently speak of a temple, but usually it is God's eternal temple in heaven to which they refer.[4] Ezekiel's vision of the temple certainly has eschatological significance, as is clear from parallels with the book of Revelation. Further, Jeremiah warns against a false faith in the temple: "Do not trust in these deceptive words, 'This is the temple of the LORD, the temple of the LORD, the temple of the LORD' " (Jer. 7:4).

An apparent exception to this view of the temple is found in the postexilic rebuilding of the temple, and particularly in Haggai's prophecy. Here—perhaps for the only time in the Bible—God commands a temple to be built (Hag. 1:7-8).

Haggai had four visions within a span of four months. The temple lay in ruins, but the people were more preoccupied with embellishing their own homes than with rebuilding God's house. In the first vision God commands them to rebuild the temple. Why? Because the people had left their first love. The temple had become the symbol of God's presence, and their neglect of it was sign and symptom of their neglect of God himself.

But in the succeeding visions, also relating to the temple, God's will is put into eschatological perspective. God says, in effect, "Do you see how this temple you are rebuilding is only a shadow of the glory of the former? But the time is coming when things will change." God says, "I will fill this house with glory; . . . and the glory of this latter house shall surpass the glory of the former" (Hag. 2:3-9, NEB). The reference here is to the eschatological future (as in other similar passages) and not to the immediate future of the physical temple, which could not (and never did) compare with the earlier, Solomonic temple.

What is the point of Haggai's prophecy, then? Simply that the people were being unfaithful to God, and God commanded the rebuilding of the temple as an act of rededication to the covenant made with Solomon.

But even here the earthly temple is not permitted to assume undue importance in itself. Immediately it is put into eternal perspective: The physical temple is only the shadow of what is to come in God's future kingdom, when God shakes heaven and earth, sea and land (Hag. 2:21-23).

Even Isaiah's sublime vision in Isaiah 6 lends no legitimacy to the earthly temple. His eyes were opened to see God on his eternal throne, in his heavenly temple. The imagery is clearly that of the celestial temple, not of the earthly one. (Compare Rev. 4:1-11.) Interestingly, the passage does not even say Isaiah was in the temple when the vision came, although we usually assume this. He may have been resting in his own house when the Lord appeared.

We see, then, in the tabernacle and the desert wandering the Old Testament counterpart of the church in history as God's pilgrim people.[5] The temple and the kingdom more truly represent Christ's eschatological kingdom, to be fulfilled in the age to come. Both the tabernacle and the temple represent God's habitation with his people. But the simpler, unpretentious, wandering tabernacle is the truer symbol of the church on earth.

Tabernacle and Church With the birth of the church the need for an actual tabernacle or temple passed away. No longer was a temple needed; there was no longer any one holy place for worship and sacrifice (Jn. 4:20-24), for the sacrifice had already been made, once for all. All that was necessary was a place to meet together as the Christian community. The most logical place was the home (Acts 2:46; 5:42). Jewish Christians continued worshiping for some time in the temple, but the practice gradually dropped off. And the temple was destroyed in A.D. 70.

It is striking that Stephen in his appeal in the temple prior to his martyrdom goes directly from a discussion of the tabernacle and the temple to his condemnation of the Jewish leaders:

Our fathers had the tent of witness in the wilderness, even as he who spoke to Moses directed him to make it, according to the pattern that he had seen. . . . So it was until the days of David, who found favor in the sight of God and asked leave to find a habitation for the God of Jacob. But it was Solomon who built a house for him. Yet the Most High does not dwell in houses made with hands. (Acts 7:44-48)

The point here seems to be the Jews' slowness of heart to recognize the true signs of God's presence. They "resist the Holy Spirit" by trusting in the physical temple, failing to see Jesus Christ as the fulfillment of both tabernacle and temple, as both priest and king. So accustomed to looking for God in stone and mortar, they do not recognize him in human flesh (Jn. 1:10-11). They have rejected Jesus Christ and are trusting in that which no more has meaning.

All of this suggests a most basic fact: *Theologically, the church does not need temples.* Church buildings are not essential to the true nature of the church. For the meaning of the tabernacle is God's habitation, and God already dwells within the human community of Christian believers. The people are the temple and the tabernacle, a tabernacle "not made with hands," a "greater and more perfect tent" of which the Mosaic tabernacle was but a copy (Heb. 9:11). Thus, theologically, church buildings are superfluous. They are not needed for priestly functions because all believers are priests and all have direct access, at whatever time and place, to the one great high priest. A church building cannot properly be "the Lord's house" because in the new covenant this title is reserved for the church *as people* (Eph. 2; 1 Tim. 3:15; Heb. 10:21). A church building cannot be a "holy place" in any special sense, for holy places no longer exist. Christianity has no holy *places*, only holy *people*.

It is hard to find biblical support for constructing church buildings. On the contrary, the teaching of Hebrews—which most clearly asserts that the sacrificial system and the priesthood have passed away so that the church now needs neither —may imply that the church should not become involved in building churches any more than it should institute a new priesthood or a new sacrifice. In any case, the early church did not build church buildings.[6]

The conclusion that the church, theologically, does not need buildings is reinforced by the distinction we have seen between tabernacle and temple. We have noted God's apparent preference for the tabernacle over the temple as the sign of his habitation with his people, for the tabernacle emphasizes God as dynamic not static, as mobile, as a God of surprises. And it thus shows God's people—the church—as mobile and flexible, as pilgrims. But the image of the temple is strikingly incompatible with the idea of a pilgrim people. There is a certain incongruity to the portable ark of the covenant resting securely within Solomon's temple. A temple cannot be moved; it can only be destroyed. It is static. And so in the Bible God does not command the church to build temples. The tabernacle is the truer sign of his presence, and even it has been fulfilled and has passed away.

So if church buildings have any justification, it can only be practical—simply a place to meet and carry on essential functions, as necessary. Beyond this, buildings become a return to the shadow of the Old Testament and a betrayal of the reality of the New.

Theologically, church buildings are at best unnecessary and at worst idolatrous. If the priesthood and the sacrificial system have passed away, so should the tabernacle. All three have ceased to be institutions and have become something alive, through the life-giving Spirit of Christ and through his Body, which we are.

Much of this is well said in the following words, quoted by John Havlik in *People-Centered Evangelism:*

The church is never a place, but always a people; never a fold but always a flock; never a sacred building but always a believing assem-

bly. The church is you who pray, not where you pray. A structure of brick or marble can no more be a church than your clothes of serge or satin can be you. There is in this world nothing sacred but man, no sanctuary of man but the soul.[7]

This is the true nature of the church. And this is what the early church experienced.

5

ARE CHURCH BUILDINGS SUPERFLUOUS?

Just think of it!

"If you had asked, 'Where is the church?' in any important city of the ancient world where Christianity had penetrated in the first century, you would have been directed to a group of worshiping people gathered in a house. There was no special building or other tangible wealth with which to associate 'church,' only people!" So wrote the late Walter Oetting in a significant little book, *The Church of the Catacombs.*[1]

Christians did not begin to build church buildings until about A.D. 200. This fact suggests that, whatever else church buildings are good for, they are not essential either for numerical growth or spiritual depth. The early church possessed both these qualities, and the church's greatest period of vitality and growth until recent times was during the first two centuries A.D. In other words, the church grew fastest when it did not have the help—or hindrance—of church buildings.

But if it is really true that church buildings are not essential either for growth or spirituality, why do churches today depend so heavily on buildings? Is it true the church suffers an "edifice complex"?

The Witness of Church Buildings Church buildings attest to five facts about the church today.

First, church buildings are *a witness to our immobility.* What is more immovable than a church building? And yet Christians are, supposedly, wayfaring pilgrims. Christians are to be a mobile people. In the Old Testament the portable tabernacle was the symbol of God's presence in community with his people, as we noted in the previous chapter. The Old Testament did not find its fulfillment in impressive church buildings but in the fleshly temple, people.

The gospel says, "Go," but our church buildings say, "Stay." The gospel says, "Seek the lost," but our churches say, "Let the lost seek the church."

Second, church buildings are *a witness to our inflexibility*. As soon as we erect a building, we cut down on our options by at least seventy-five per cent. Once the building is up and in use, the church program and budget are largely determined. The Sunday morning service allows the direct participation of only a few—dictated by the sanctuary layout. Basically the services will be a matter of one person speaking to all the rest, and this one person will be set apart and recognized as a professional —dictated by the platform arrangement. Communication will be one-way (if that is communication)—preacher to people—dictated by architecture and the PA system. And so on. Architecture petrifies program.

The problem, at heart, is not one of poor planning. It is a matter of the inherent limitations of church buildings. Buildings are, by nature, inflexible and encourage inflexibility—or worse, stagnation.[2] After a number of years as an urban minister in Los Angeles, Lawrence Carter said it this way, "At present, city churches are slaves to their brick and mortar at a time when the Church needs to be flexible, adaptable, and relevant to the very real needs, sorrows, and aspirations of a rapidly changing urban population."[3] And the same could be said of the majority of suburban and small-town churches.

Third, church buildings are *a witness to our lack of fellowship.* Church buildings may be worshipful places, but usually they are not friendly places. They are uncomfortable and impersonal. Church buildings are not made for fellowship, for *koinonia* in the biblical sense. Homes are. And it was in homes that early Christians met to worship (Acts 2:42; 5:42). Church buildings are made for worship, but worship without fellowship becomes something cold and divorced from reality.

In probably ninety per cent of all church buildings the sanctuary seating consists of wooden pews arranged in rows and screwed securely to the floor. The pews are arranged to make it nearly impossible for a worshiper to directly see the face of any other worshiper. It is as though the ideal would be to put each worshiper in his own private isolation booth so he could see only the minister and not be distracted by other people. But if we are to worship the Lord together, we need to be together. To communicate with each other as we worship, we must be able to see each other. We must be able to see the attentive face, the tearful eye, the quiet smile that tell us something is happening and let us enter into worship *together*.

Many modern congregations have sensed this lack of fellowship in the church and so have added something called a "fellowship hall." But how frequently do we attain, either in the fellowship hall, the sanctuary or the Sunday school class, anything that truly can be called fellowship? True *koinonia,* real biblical Christian fellowship such as experienced by the early Christians, is lacking in most churches today.[4]

And so a stranger may attend a Christian church for weeks and never encounter the winsome, warm, loving fellowship that draws a person to Christ. Such a situation would simply have been impossible in A.D. 100.

Fourth, church buildings are *a witness to our pride.* We insist that our church structures must be beautiful and well-appointed—which usually means expensive—and justify this on the grounds that God deserves the best. But such thinking may be little more than the rationalizing of carnal pride.

Or we say, perhaps, that, after all, we are ambassadors for the King of kings, who is abundantly rich. True. But this does not justify spending vast resources to build embassies. We may forget that our king is at war, and we are called to be his witnessing soldiers.

We have other justifications for our expensive temples. We may, for instance, feel that we must have beautiful buildings in order to draw sinners to the church and thus to Christ. But two things are wrong here. First, the concept is wrong. The church is to seek the sinner, not vice versa. Second, the motivation is wrong. We try to attract sinners by appealing to pride ("We certainly are pleased and honored to have Mrs. Hackett, little Sandra's mother, visiting our Sunday school today, and we hope both she and Mr. Hackett will be able to come next Sunday . . ."). This was not Christ's approach. Too often our churches end up competing with each other on the architectural plane. This is evangelism at its worst.

We often say that our church buildings must be in harmony —in style and value—with the architecture of the community. But this idea may merely be a brand of conformity to the world. A gospel with New Testament dynamic does not need to make a good impression on the world through the appeal of an attractive building. That is rather like wrapping a diamond in tin foil to help it sell. In fact, a fine church building may simply attract the Pharisees and repel the poor. That has, after all, happened before in church history.

Since when is it the church's task to melt chameleon-like into the surrounding environment? The church is to stand for Christ *against* man-made culture. This should be true even in architecture. If buildings are to be built, let them speak of God, not of middle-class bourgeois values.

Finally, church buildings are *a witness to our class divisions.* The early church was composed of rich and poor, Jew and Greek, black and white, ignorant and educated. But our modern church buildings advertise to the world that this is not true today. A sociologist can take a casual look at ten church buildings and their denominational brand names and then predict with high accuracy the education, income, occupations and social position of the majority of their respective members. In the light of the New Testament, this ought not to be.

But, in a less sophisticated way, the new family in the community does the same thing as the sociologist. The family goes for a drive and looks over the neighborhood church buildings. They choose one that looks like "their kind"—one that will contain people of approximately the same income, education, politics and color as themselves. In most cases, a careful look at the building is enough to tell them whether they will "feel at home" there. Of course, occasionally they may be fooled by a lower-class church that is moving up in the world and has just completed a building program.

The fault here, of course, lies much deeper than mere architecture. But the building is a *witness.* It is a signpost telling the world of the church's class consciousness and exclusiveness.

Our church buildings, then, witness to the *immobility, inflexibility, lack of fellowship, pride* and *class divisions* in the modern church.

What Should Be Done? What then should be done? Should we simply abandon the use of church buildings?

For many churches, this would be the best solution. A different kind of architecture is not enough. Remember, during its most vital 150 years, the Christian church never even heard of church buildings. In those days it was mobile, flexible, friendly, humble, inclusive—and growing like mad!

We could recommend less radical solutions—less building-centered programs, more visitation evangelism, simpler architecture. But why? Why continue building temples? Why not simply do away with them? Traditional church buildings are unnecessary in an urban world and are often a hindrance to biblical Christianity.

Of course, to suggest that church buildings are unnecessary

luxuries immediately raises a storm of protest:

"What would be done with all that property?" Christ's words perhaps suggest a response for a church with "great possessions": "Go, sell what you possess and give to the poor, . . . and come, follow me" (Mt. 19:21).

"But where would Christians meet?" In homes, as did the early Christians.[5] We would go back to "the church in your house" (Philem. 2).

"But houses are too small!" Only if the church is too big. Divide the congregation into groups of twelve to fifteen people. This would facilitate fellowship and allow the members to get acquainted with each other. It would be a refreshing experience!

"But we need large-group corporate worship." True—as I argue in chapter 8. But it is sufficient for the congregation to rent a small hall or garage where it can meet for corporate worship and training once or twice a week, and not spend hundreds of thousands of dollars to provide a large sanctuary that is used only five or six hours weekly.[6]

"But people would not be attracted to a garage or storefront." Well, there are two kinds of people—those who are committed to Christ and those who are not. Those really committed to Christ and his church will meet anywhere. Those who are not, it is true, probably would not flock to a dingy garage or humble storefront. But this is immaterial if the church is a missionary community and if the basic unit is the small Bible-study group. In this case, evangelism happens outside of "church." Hence there is no concern or reason to attract the uncommitted to the place of worship. Once they have met Christ, they will come.

"But a garage or storefront would be too small." That depends on the church's *objective.* If the goal is to bring an ever-larger number of people together in one place, then indeed a small rented location would not do. If the goal is the growth of the Body of Christ, however, a superchurch is not necessary.

Healthy growth is growth by division. Let the church form two separate congregations when it outgrows its facilities. Perhaps a voluntary limit of 100 or so should be set by a local group before it divides in two.

"But this would mean churches of only 50 to 100 members. That is too small to carry on a full church program." True—if we must have a men's organization, a women's organization, a children's organization, a youth program, a senior citizen's club, Sunday school, midweek prayer service, training programs, five boards and ten committees (about par for the ecclesiastical course). But with a flexible program that is not edifice-centered, this is not necessary. The basic unit of organization becomes the small group, and the thesis is that every essential organizational function of the church can be effectively carried out through these groups.

To be realistic, one must recognize the great diversity that exists from one local church to another. It is conceivable that one edifice-bound church might sell its building and still continue in an institutional rut, never experiencing real spiritual renewal. On the other hand, some churches with considerable property apparently know how to see such facilities as functional rather than sacred and are alive and spiritually dynamic. This indicates that the edifice complex is often as much conceptual as material.

Four Categories of Churches Local churches may theoretically be divided into four categories with reference to buildings. In each case, the needed course of action may be different.

1. *The Body Church.* This type is closest to the New Testament experience. It holds no property and needs none. It arranges its worship gatherings according to available space in homes, schools, rented halls or other facilities. Its structure is largely organic, based on a network of small groups bound together by large-group corporate worship experiences.

Such a church can live and grow indefinitely, having a profound impact on society through a continuous process of cell division and multiplication. Its structure is seen as normal, not provisional or transitional. No plans need be made for a building; such a church is spiritually complete.

2. *The Cathedral Church.* Regardless of the size of its building, such a church really sees the building as *the church,* and it is the building which determines the church's whole program and lifestyle. Members of this type of church can only think that a church without a building would be like a body without a skeleton. The building defines everything, from finances to discipleship. I recently heard of a little church which had difficulty squeezing out $1,500 for foreign missions while it was busy raising $10,000 to pave the parking lot! Little wonder the church is small.

This kind of church has missed the biblical understanding of the Body of Christ. Whether it has thirty members or one thousand, it is in spiritual danger. Such a church should seriously consider ridding itself of its property and shifting to a more person-centered lifestyle. Failing such a miracle, a concerned nucleus within the church should form itself into an organic cell to begin to rediscover the living church.

3. *The Tabernacle Church.* This church has a building, but the building is strictly secondary and functional. It is not a "holy place" in any inherent sense, but is seen as a facility to be used to extend the kingdom of God. The building may be large or small, simple or elaborate. The important thing is that it is functional. It is built for flexibility and multiple use. Its style represents proper stewardship of time and money and says something true and positive about the gospel.

I call this the Tabernacle Church not because of the size or structure of the building but because the building is seen as a tabernacle or tent, provisional and temporary, to be used or dispensed with as circumstances demand. (Some so-called Gospel Tabernacles are in reality Cathedral Churches while some more elaborate and esthetic structures are really functioning as tabernacles.)

One can make little criticism of such a church as long as it continues to function in this way and does not drift into a cathedral mentality.

4. *The Phantom Church.* This final type prides itself on having no building. The problem is, it has very little structure of any kind! It is like a Rorschach ink blot: Each person makes what he wants of it. Its nebulous existence is based on occasional, almost impromptu, gatherings and, for all its talk about community, it may be highly individualistic. *It has not yet become a body* of mutual responsibility and organic interrelatedness. Since it lacks structure, one of two things may happen. It may simply evaporate like a fog bank in the sun. Or a strong personality may emerge who imposes his own brand of structure and converts the group into an organization.

This is not a biblical type, obviously, and cannot continue indefinitely. But superficially it may at first look identical to the Body Church. Ideally, such an amorphous group should seek and find the biblical pattern of the church as an organic community and become more literally the Body of Christ.

To sum up: While the Body Church most clearly duplicates the New Testament experience, the Tabernacle Church may be a legitimate incarnation of the community of God's people in some contexts.

Where Do We Fit? Where does my church, or yours, fit into this classification? A little analysis should reveal whether one's church is really faithful to the biblical understanding of God's people or whether it has been captured by the edifice complex.

How can one tell? It seems to me that any church which

spends more on buildings than on outreach
holds all its gatherings only in "the church"
puts construction before missions and evangelism

refuses to use its building for anything other than "sacred" functions
measures spirituality by the number of human bodies present within the four walls

has an edifice complex and is almost totally ignorant of what the Bible means by *the church.* In such a case some hard thinking and reappraisal are necessary preparation for setting some specific goals to right the situation. As a starter, such a church might set a goal of annually increasing its financial giving for foreign missions, social ministries, evangelism and similar needs by ten per cent *beyond* the percentage increase of the total church budget until at least half of the church's giving goes to help others.[7] More fundamentally, such a church needs to re-examine its whole lifestyle of community, service and worship along the lines suggested throughout this book.

Hugh Steven recounts how, at the beginning of the Jesus Movement in southern California, Chuck Smith's Calvary Chapel faced a crisis over whether or not to let barefooted hippie types trample all over its beautiful carpet. The saints had been assured that oily bare feet would ruin the rug. Here was a crisis over priorities: people or property? The church decided in favor of people, and hundreds of barefooted youths came to Christ.[8]

Argentina's Juan Carlos Ortiz, pastor of a growing church in Buenos Aires, tells how he shut down the church building for a month to see if the church could survive under persecution conditions. What happened? The church continued to function normally. Why? Because it was structured like a body, made up of a whole network of informal contacts and small cell groups; the building was secondary. During the month financial contributions were handled through the small groups. Says Ortiz, "More money came in during that month than ever before!"[9]

In these days, so parallel to New Testament times, the traditional church building is an anachronism the church can no longer afford. This is not to say no community of believers should ever hold property. But it is to say that any property, any building, should be held lightly, and should be an expression of a clear biblical understanding of the true nature of the church. Any building so held must be *functional*—a means, not an end. The road back to the Middle Ages is all too easy to take.

6

MUST THE PASTOR BE A SUPERSTAR?

Meet Pastor Jones, Superstar.

He can preach, counsel, evangelize, administrate, conciliate, communicate and sometimes even integrate. He can also raise the budget.

He handles Sunday morning better than any quizmaster on weekday TV. He is better with words than most political candidates. As a scholar he surpasses many seminary professors. No church social function would be complete without him.

His church, of course, Counts Itself Fortunate. Alas, not many churches can boast such talent.

I confess my admiration, perhaps slightly tinged with envy. Not because of the talent, really, the sheer ability. But for the success, the accomplishment. Here is a man who faithfully preaches the Word, sees lives transformed by Christ, sees his church growing. What sincere evangelical minister would not like to be in his shoes? Not to mention his parsonage.

I think of all the struggling, mediocre pastors, looking on with holy envy (if there be such), measuring their own performance by Pastor Jones' success and dropping another notch into discouragement or, perhaps, self-condemnation.

For after all, the problem is plain, isn't it? The church needs more qualified pastors, better training. More alertness to guiding those talented young men God may be calling into "the ministry." Better talent scouting to find the superstars.

But—what if?

What if the problem is not really the lack of superstars? What if there is something basically wrong with the traditional concept of ministry in the church?

Is the problem really a lack of ecclesiastical superstars? Or do we have unbiblical concepts of what the church really is?

Can it be that our structures quench the Spirit?

Take Pastor Jones' church. There is Bill S——, who has unusual speaking ability. Won a debate championship in high school. He would be capable of preaching—but nobody ever thought of that. He's an usher.

Then there is John M——. Nice guy. Everyone's friend. People naturally go to him with their problems; he has a knack for listening; he even listens with his eyes. With a little training and encouragement he could have a real ministry of the healing of persons. He would also need a little more time: He's on three church committees.

Or Bob B——, accountant. Naturally, he is church finance chairman, and he does an excellent job. No one knows he is also something of a self-taught Bible scholar—a seemingly superfluous talent.

In fact, looking into the lives of the several hundred members of Pastor Jones' church, we make a startling discovery: Every one of Pastor Jones' talents is equalled or surpassed by someone in the membership. A wealth of gifts lies buried because these talents are seemingly not needed. True, no one in the church comes close to being a superstar like Pastor Jones. True also, for each talent there is probably a corresponding hang-up. But maybe God could use those talents and heal those hang-ups if we thought differently about ministry.

What about the early church? Paul had a dramatic put-down for the superstar idea:

There are varieties of gifts, but the same Spirit. There are varieties of service, but the same Lord. There are many forms of work, but all of them, in all men, are the work of the same God. In each of us the Spirit is manifested in one particular way, for some useful purpose. . . .

For Christ is like a single body with its many limbs and organs, which, many as they are, together make up one body. . . .

A body is not one single organ, but many. Suppose the foot should say, "Because I am not a hand, I do not belong to the body," it does belong to the body none the less. . . . But, in fact, God appointed each limb and organ to its own place in the body, as he chose. If the whole were one single organ, there would not be a body at all; in fact, however, there are many different organs, but one body. . . .

Now you are Christ's body, and each of you a limb or organ of it. Within our community God has appointed, in the first place apostles, in the second place prophets, thirdly teachers; then miracle-workers, then those who have gifts of healing, or ability to help others or power to guide them, or the gift of ecstatic utterance of various kinds. (1 Cor. 12:4-7, 12, 14-15, 18-20, 27-28, NEB)

Got that? "If the whole were one single organ, there would not be a body at all." If the pastor is a superstar, then the church is an audience, not a body.

I had read many times what the Bible says about the gifts of the Spirit. I never understood. I could not figure out why the whole thing really did not make any sense for the church *today*. It did not seem to fit. Could it really be that these words were written only for the early church, as some affirm?

Then it struck me. These words are for the church in every age, but to the church today they seem superfluous. For we have got all the gifts organized. We do not need the Spirit (Dreadful thing to say!) to stir up gifts of ministry. We just need superstars to make the organization *Go*.

So we depend on our structures and our superstars. And we *know* the system *works*—just look what the superstars are doing in their superchurches! We have the statistics and the buildings and the budgets to prove it.

There is only one problem.

There are not enough superstars to go around. Thousands of churches, but only hundreds of superstars.

Thank God for the superstars! They are of all men most fortunate. But the church of Jesus Christ cannot run on superstars, and God never intended that it should. There just are not that many, actually or potentially, and there never will be. God does not promise the church an affluence of superstars. But he does promise to provide all necessary leadership through the gifts of the Spirit (Eph. 4:1-16). If a denomination must depend on pastoral superstars for growth, there is something drastically wrong with its structure and, more fundamentally, with its understanding of the church.

Pray the Lord of the harvest that he send forth reapers, not foremen.

Cheer up, discouraged pastor, discouraged "layman." The problem really is not your own inadequacy. Go reread the New Testament with a question: After Peter and Paul, where are the superstars? How did the early church "make it" without our organization, cathedrals or superstars?

Young Ralph C—— has been thinking of going into "the ministry," but he hesitates because he knows he is not a superstar. (What if your churches did not require superstars?)

Chuck Y—— is 38 and has a good job with an electronics firm; I know him well. He is frustrated and would like some kind of significant ministry—something more challenging than a Sunday school class. But he thinks he would have to quit his job and go to seminary first. (What if more pastors had secular employment and on-the-job training, as in the New Testament?)

Let's face it! James and John and Philip and Bartholomew could never have made it in the twentieth century. At least not within *our* churches. Neither would Epaphras, Mark, Aristarchus, Demas or Luke, some friends of Paul (Philem. 23). These were no superstars in their day; they only look that way through the mists of history and tradition. But they were used of the Spirit, each according to his gifts. Their congregations had not heard that they had to have a superstar up front, so all believers worked together building up the community of faith. There were many ministers in each congregation. Like a body, each part exercised its proper function.

Do our structures quench the Spirit?

"So, for the sake of your tradition, you have made void the word of God" (Mt. 15:6). The Word of God is not bound—unless we bind it. What, then, does the unfettered Word say about the church?

It is time to go back to the Word to find a biblical ecclesiology, a biblical concept of the church compatible with the new stirrings of the Spirit in our day.

Let both the Spirit *and* the Bride say, "Come."

PART 3: BIBLICAL MATERIAL FOR NEW WINESKINS

7

THE FELLOWSHIP OF THE HOLY SPIRIT

True Christian fellowship—what the Greek New Testament calls *koinonia*—is the Spirit's gift to the church. Yet this fellowship is critically lacking in much of the institutional church today. And this lack goes to the very heart of the impotence, rigidity and seeming irrelevance of much of the modern church.

The church is especially under attack today for its rigid institutionalism, its "morphological fundamentalism." Critics call for more relevant structures for the church and for a new ecclesiology. I would like to suggest that the New Testament concept of *the koinonia of the Holy Spirit* offers a helpful starting point in this quest for more intimate, less institutionalized structures for the church's life.

A Fellowship Crisis The church today is suffering a fellowship crisis. It is simply not experiencing nor demonstrating that "fellowship of the Holy Spirit" (2 Cor. 13:14) that marked the New Testament church. In a world of big, impersonal institutions, the church often looks like just another big, impersonal institution. The church is highly organized just at the time when her members are caring less about organization and more about community. One seldom finds within the institutionalized church today that winsome intimacy among people where masks are dropped, honesty prevails and there is that sense of communication and community beyond the human—where there is literally the fellowship of and in the Holy Spirit.

The considerable popularity of Keith Miller's *The Taste of New Wine* was largely due, I believe, to the fact that Miller put his finger precisely on this lack in the church. He struck a responsive chord with thousands of sincere Christians when he observed,

Our churches are filled with people who outwardly look contented and at peace but inwardly are crying out for someone to love them . . . just as they are–confused, frustrated, often frightened, guilty, and often unable to communicate even within their own families. But the other *people in the church* look *so happy and contented that one seldom has the courage to admit his own deep needs before such a self-sufficient group as the average church meeting appears to be.*[1]

This unintentioned duplicity is an almost inevitable result of current institutional patterns of church organization. It is a description of the church without *koinonia.*

Koinonia is, of course, but one aspect of the church's total being. The New Testament church lived by witness, service and fellowship. All three are essential for the church to be faithful. The church must preach and teach, and it must serve —following the example of Christ.

But *koinonia* is essential both for effective proclamation and for relevant serving. *Koinonia* is the church abiding in the Vine, that it may bear much fruit. It is the Body becoming "joined and knit together," upbuilding itself in love, so that the individual gifts of the Spirit may be manifest in the world (Eph. 4:16). Often both the church's preaching and service have suffered simply for lack of true *koinonia.*

But what, specifically, is the *koinonia* of the Holy Spirit? And what does it tell us about church structure in our day?

What Is the "Fellowship of the Holy Spirit"? In 2 Corinthians 13:14 Paul prays that "the fellowship [*koinonia*] of the Holy

Spirit" may be with the Corinthian believers. And in Philippians 2:1 Paul speaks of the "fellowship [*koinonia*] in the Spirit."

Two dimensions are implied in these passages: the vertical dimension of the believer's fellowship with God and the horizontal dimension of his *koinonia* with other believers through the Holy Spirit. It is critical that these two aspects be held together and understood together. The New Testament idea of *koinonia* is not fully understood until we grasp the significance of the horizontal and vertical dimensions *together.*

At first we may see here only the vertical dimension of fellowship with God through the Holy Spirit. But the horizontal dimension is also very much present, and perhaps even primary: the fellowship among Christians which is the gift of the Spirit. As James Reid has written about 2 Corinthians 13:14, "This does not mean fellowship with the Spirit. It is a fellowship with God which he shares through the indwelling Spirit with those who are members of the body of Christ. *The fellowship of the Holy Spirit is the true description of the church.*"[2]

Much has been written about the meaning and implications of the word *koinonia.* Such discussion, however, has emphasized primarily the horizontal dimension, the fellowship of Christians with each other. But it is the vertical dimension which supplies the basic content to the whole idea of *koinonia*. *Koinonia* in the church must start with the fellowship of the Holy Spirit, or it lacks its New Testament dynamic. Hendrik Kraemer has well said in his *Theology of the Laity,* "The fellowship (*koinonia*) with and in Jesus Christ and the Spirit is the creative ground and sustainer of the fellowship (*koinonia*) of the believers with each other."[3] The spiritual communion and fellowship in the church which truly is *koinonia* is something given by the Spirit; it is more than a function of our humanity. It partakes of the supernatural.

Two things, then, the fellowship of the Holy Spirit emphatically is *not*:

1. *It is not that superficial social fellowship which the very word* fellowship *often denotes in our churches today.* Such "fellowship" is generally no more supernatural than the weekly Kiwanis or Rotary club meeting. Most of what passes for fellowship in the church—whatever its value—is something distinctly less than *koinonia*. It is "cheap fellowship," parallel to Bonhoeffer's "cheap grace." At best, it is a friendly fraternizing—appealing, but easily duplicated outside the church. Biblical *koinonia,* however, is unique to the church of Jesus Christ.

Typical church "fellowship" seldom reaches the level of *koinonia* because *koinonia* is neither understood, expected nor sought. Consequently there are few or no suitable structures for *koinonia* in the church. The church today has become accustomed to a pleasant, superficial sociality which is at best a cut-rate substitute for *koinonia.*

2. *On the other hand,* koinonia *is not simply some mystical communion that exists without reference to the structure of the church.* We may talk in abstract terms about "the fellowship of the church," as though it were something that automatically, and almost by definition, binds believers together. But the abstract concept is hollow apart from the actual gathering together of believers at a particular point in time and space. We cannot escape this, not on this earth. Christ himself emphasized the necessity of being together when he said, "Where two or three are gathered in my name, there am I in the midst of them" (Mt. 18:20). One can have fellowship with God when one is alone, and in any place, for God is spirit. *But one cannot have fellowship with another believer who is not present,* despite our mystical language. The fellowship of the Holy Spirit is not some ethereal power that spiritually binds believers together while they are physically separated. Rather, it is that deep spiritual community in Christ which believers experience when they gather together as the church of Christ.

More positively, we can describe the fellowship of the Holy Spirit in the following terms:

1. *The* koinonia *of the Holy Spirit is that fellowship among believers which the Holy Spirit gives.* It is precisely that experience of a deeper communion, of a supernatural intercommunication, that perhaps every believer occasionally has felt in the presence of other believers.[4] Its basis is the oneness that Christians share in Christ. A shared faith, a shared salvation and a shared divine nature are the roots of *koinonia.* The basic idea of the word *koinonia* is, in fact, that of something held in common.

2. *It is the fellowship of Christ with his disciples.* Jesus spent three years living and working in intimate fellowship with twelve men. As Robert Coleman observes, "He actually spent more time with His disciples than with everybody else in the world put together. He ate with them, slept with them, and talked with them for the most part of His entire active ministry."[5] These men not only learned from Christ; they shared a depth of community that was the prototype of the *koinonia* of the early church. It is interesting that in the midst of Christ's important discourse during the Last Supper three disciples felt free to interrupt with comments or questions (Jn. 14:5, 8, 22). Together they were experiencing the fellowship of the Holy Spirit.

3. *It is the fellowship of the early church,* as recorded in the book of Acts. The first Christians knew an unusual unity, oneness of purpose, common love and mutual concern—in other words, *koinonia.* This was more than either the immediate joy of conversion or the knowledge of shared beliefs. It was an atmosphere, a spiritual environment, that grew among the first believers as they prayed, learned and worshiped together in their own homes (Acts 2:42-46; 5:42).

4. *It is the earthly counterpart and foretaste of the eternal fellowship of heaven.* The joy of heaven is the freedom of eternal communion with God and fellow believers, without earthly limitations. As the earthly model of this heavenly reality, *koinonia* in the church shares the same spiritual nature as life in heaven; it

is not qualitatively different. But it suffers the necessary limitations of the flesh and of space and time. Thus *koinonia* in the church is neither continuous nor universal. Rather, it is interrupted, partial, local—and necessarily so. It is limited and affected by physical factors, but its essential reality is not of this world.

5. *It is analogous to the unity, fellowship and communion between Christ and the Father.* A parallel exists between the communion of the Trinity and the *koinonia* of believers among themselves and with God. Christ's prayer in John 17 is especially suggestive here. Jesus asks that his disciples "may be one, as we are one." More generally, he prays for all future Christians that "they all be one: as thou, Father, art in me, and I in thee, so also may they be in us, that the world may believe that thou didst send me" (Jn. 17:11, 21, NEB). *Koinonia* is the fulfillment of this prayer in the church and thus a manifestation in space and time of the communion of the Holy Trinity. It is a supernatural intersharing between the Persons of the Godhead and the church on earth, inseparably involving both the vertical and horizontal dimensions. Christ wanted his followers to be one in their *koinonia*—one not only with God but also with each other.

Such *koinonia* is the gift of the Holy Spirit. But is the church then powerless to create or nurture this fellowship? Or may church structures provide the conditions for the fellowship of the Holy Spirit?

Daniel J. Fleming makes the following point in his book *Living as Comrades:* "The fashioning and preservation of this *koinonia* . . . is the peculiar work of the Holy Spirit. But . . . we can help or hinder that consummation by the degree to which we consciously endeavor to enter into community with fellow human beings."[6] And that applies to the church as well as to individual believers.

The Bible is largely silent as to specific structures for the church. The New Testament contains no Sinai revelations as to the "pattern of the tabernacle." We are free to create those structures most conducive to the mission and need of the church in our time, within the broad outlines of the biblical vision of the church.[7] And the very idea of the *koinonia* of the Holy Spirit may have something very significant to say about such structures.

Implications for Church Structure At Pentecost the Holy Spirit gave the infant church, among other things, the gift of *koinonia*. This is the only explanation for the early Christian community described in Acts. The creation of genuine fellowship is an integral part of the work of the Holy Spirit. In this sense the Holy Spirit's work in the individual believer cannot be separated from what he is doing within the church—the church not as so many individual believers but precisely as a community of faith.

Failure to see this vital interconnection between the individual and group aspects of the Spirit's working weakens our understanding both of the individual believer and of the church. It is, first, to view the believer's spiritual development in too much of an individualized, separated sense, as though Christians grow best in isolation. And second, it misses an element of basic significance for the structure and ministry of the church: The church provides the context for spiritual growth by sharing *together* a fellowship which is at once the *gift* of the Spirit and the *environment* in which he may operate.

Thus a natural connection exists, I suggest, between the fellowship of the Holy Spirit and church structure. The nature of this *koinonia* in fact contains several implications for the form of the church.

First of all, as already noted, the fellowship of the Holy Spirit is a function of the church gathered, not of the church scattered. The obvious implication for church structure: *The church must make sufficient provision to be gathered together if it is to experience* koinonia. *Koinonia* requires being together in one place at one time under the direction of the Holy Spirit. We can talk about the fellowship of the Holy Spirit as being solely a spiritual reality, ignoring the space-time limitations, but this is meaningless. The fact is that the fellowship of the Holy Spirit—New Testament *koinonia* in the church—*requires,* as an *absolute necessity,* physical proximity. The church does not experience the fellowship of the Holy Spirit if it does not meet together in an atmosphere conducive to the Spirit's working.

Second, the fellowship of the Holy Spirit naturally suggests communication. Communion without communication would be a contradiction in terms. Thus a second implication for church structure: *The church must meet together in a way that permits and encourages communication among the members.*

This fact immediately raises questions about traditional structures of worship in the institutional church. Whatever its value, the traditional church worship service is not well designed for intercommunication, for fellowship. It is designed, both by liturgy and architecture, principally for a one-way kind of communication, pulpit-to-pew. Indeed, communication between two worshipers during the church services is considered rude and outside the spirit of worship. As Alan Watts commented caustically, "Participants sit in rows looking at the back of each other's necks, and are in communication only with the leader."[8]

The traditional church service is not the proper structure for experiencing the fellowship of the Holy Spirit. And we may say by extension that *no* church meeting is conducive to *koinonia* if it is based on a one-way, leader-to-group kind of communication, whether it be prayer meeting, Sunday school class or Bible study hour. *Koinonia* appears and flourishes only in structures that allow and encourage communication.

And since *koinonia* involves the vertical dimension as well as the horizontal, this communication also implies communion with God; in other words, prayer is part of *koinonia.*

A third implication for wineskins involves the element of

freedom. Paul gives us the principle, "Where the Spirit of the Lord is, there is freedom" (2 Cor. 3:17). The Holy Spirit is the liberator, the freer. The freedom of the Spirit and the *koinonia* of the Spirit go together. Where there is *koinonia* there is also freedom and openness, an atmosphere which permits "speaking the truth in love" (Eph. 4:15). True *koinonia* can be experienced only where there is the freedom of the Spirit.

The implication for structure: *The church must provide structures which are sufficiently informal and intimate to permit the freedom of the Spirit.* There must be a sense of the unexpected and the unprogrammed when believers come together, the excitement of the unpredictable, a freedom from set patterns and forms. Frequently in an informal and rather loosely structured gathering of believers one finds a greater openness to God's moving and thus a greater likelihood that the fellowship of the Holy Spirit will be experienced.

This is not, of course, to argue against the proper use of planning, form and liturgy. Believers need those times of solemn corporate worship in which the High and Holy God is honored with dignity and reverence. But in the midst of the dignity and reverence many a lonely believer inwardly cries out for the warm, healing touch of *koinonia.* Believers need to know by experience that the Most High God is also the Most Nigh God (Is. 57:15). If traditional corporate worship is not regularly supplemented with informal opportunities for *koinonia,* believers easily drift into a practical deism while the church becomes the sacred guardian of a powerless form of godliness. On the other hand, form and liturgy take on new meaning for Christians who are living and growing in *koinonia.*

Robert Raines makes essentially the same point in his book *New Life in the Church*:

The church must foster and sustain the conditions in which koinonia *can be known. This cannot be done for most people simply through morning worship. Worship is indispensable as the weekly meeting of the Christian community. But it is effective only as the total sharing of all the people of the friendship in Christ they have known between Sundays.*[9]

Finally, the fellowship of the Holy Spirit suggests a learning situation. Jesus said that when the Holy Spirit came he would "teach you all things, and bring to your remembrance all that I have said to you" (Jn. 14:26). He would testify of Christ and guide the believers into new truth (Jn. 15:26; 16:13). The Holy Spirit came to teach, to reveal the Word.

Since it is the same Spirit of God who inbreathes and speaks through the Holy Scriptures (2 Tim. 3:16; 2 Pet. 1:21), and since these Scriptures themselves testify of Christ (Jn. 5:39), it follows that the *koinonia* of the Holy Spirit is naturally related to Bible study. We in fact find the two thus connected in the early church, which devoted itself "to the apostles' teaching and *koinonia*" (Acts 2:42).

The implication for church structure here: *Church structure must provide for Bible study in the context of community.* When Christians meet jointly with the objective task of Bible study before them and under the direction of the Holy Spirit, they experience *koinonia* that has life-changing results. They are touched by the Spirit and the Word. They find that the way to learn of Christ is in the context of a community of believers taught by the Holy Spirit.

The idea of the *koinonia* of the Holy Spirit, then, suggests that the church should provide structures in which (1) believers gather together, (2) intercommunication is encouraged, (3) an informal atmosphere allows the freedom of the Spirit and (4) direct Bible study is central.

Most contemporary church patterns and structures clearly do not meet these criteria. But there is one structure which does: some form of small group. It is my conviction that *the* koinonia *of the Holy Spirit is most likely to be experienced when Christians meet together informally in small-group fellowships.*

The small group can meet the above criteria. It brings believers together at one point in time and space. Its smallness and intimacy allow a high degree of communion and intercommunication. It does not require formal structuring; it can maintain order without stifling the informality and openness conducive to the freedom of the Spirit. And finally, it offers an ideal context for in-depth Bible study.

The early church experienced the *koinonia* of the Holy Spirit. We know also that the early Christians met together in small groups in homes. Coincidence? Or does the very idea of the *koinonia* of the Holy Spirit not suggest the need for some kind of small group fellowships as a basic structure within the church?

George Webber in his discussion of small groups in *The Congregation in Mission* notes, "No relationship of love can develop unless there are structures in which it can grow."[10] *Koinonia* in the Holy Spirit grows when there are structures to nourish it.

8

THE PEOPLE OF GOD

Another perspective for viewing the church is to see it as the result of God's cosmic purpose in calling and preparing a special people. And this also relates to wineskins.

Adam and Eve were to "be fruitful and multiply, and fill the earth," becoming a people (Gen. 1:28).[1] God's promise to Abraham was, "I will make of you a great nation" (Gen. 12:2) —and he did. God chose the children of Israel, redeeming them from Egypt, saying, "I will take you for my people, and I will be your God" (Ex. 6:7; compare Deut. 7:6). This theme echoes consistently through the Old Testament.

Moving into the New Testament, we learn that the people of God finds its center and basis in Jesus Christ. The unfaithfulness of God's people in the Old Testament did not thwart God's plan. God is still calling out and preparing his people, not principally the biological Israel but the new and true Israel, the church.[2] John the Baptist came "in the spirit and power of Elijah," his ministry "to make ready for the Lord a people prepared" (Lk. 1:17).

Paul was deeply conscious of God's plan to prepare a people on the basis of faith. Christ "gave himself for us to redeem us from all iniquity and to purify for himself a people of his own who are zealous for good deeds" (Tit. 2:14; compare Rom. 9:25-26; 2 Cor. 6:16). The same fact is cited by James (Acts 15:14), John (Rev. 21:3) and the writer to the Hebrews (Heb.

8:10). Peter says, "You are a chosen race, a royal priesthood, a holy nation, God's own people. . . . Once you were no people but now you are God's people; once you had not received mercy but now you have received mercy" (1 Pet. 2:9-10). This is the "new covenant" of which Jeremiah spoke, in which God says, "I will be their God, and they shall be my people" (Jer. 31:33).

But precisely what does it mean, biblically, to be a *people*? And how should the church be structured in order to experience this reality of peoplehood?

The Biblical Basis The idea of *a people* has rich biblical and especially Old Testament roots. Biblical Greek uses the word *laos* in referring to the church as a people. This word (from which we get *laity*) occurs over 2,000 times in the Septuagint, usually translating the Hebrew word *'am*. *Laos* is the word commonly used for Israel as God's people; "it serves to emphasize the special and privileged religious position of this people as the people of God."[3] In the Old Testament, *laos* "is the national society of Israel according to its religious basis and distinction."[4]

In the New Testament, *laos* occurs some 140 times. It is the word both Paul and Peter use to describe the church as a people, as the new Israel. Thus in the New Testament "a new and figurative Christian concept arises along with the old biological and historical view and crowds it out."[5]

It is this forming of a people which provides the basis for the church's mission of service and proclamation. *As a people, the church is itself the verification of the message it proclaims,* or else the betrayal of that message. As Mennonite scholar John Howard Yoder notes, "The work of God is the calling of a people, whether in the Old Covenant or the New. . . . That men are called together to a new social wholeness is itself the work of God which gives meaning to history, from which both personal conversion . . . and missionary instrumentalities are derived."[6] Yoder continues,

Pragmatically it is self-evident that there can be no procedure of proclamation without a community, distinct from the rest of society, to do the proclaiming. Pragmatically it is just as clear that there can be no evangelistic call addressed to a person inviting him to enter into a new kind of fellowship and learning if there is not such a body of persons, again distinct from the totality of society, to whom he can come and with and from whom he can learn. . . . If it is not the case that there are in a given place men of various characters and origins who have been brought together in Jesus Christ, then there is not in that place the new humanity and in that place the gospel is not true. If, on the other hand, this miracle of new creation has occurred, then all the verbalizations and interpretations whereby this brotherhood communicates itself to the world around it are simply explications of the fact of its presence.[7]

The church is constituted a people just as an individual is constituted a child of God—by grace through faith in Jesus Christ. The converted individual becomes part of a transformed people. And the working out of this reality always produces a church with New Testament dynamic, unless stifled by unbiblical traditions.

Biblically, we can distinguish at least five characteristics of the people of God:

1. *The church is a chosen people.* The emphasis here is on the fact of God's sovereignty and initiative; it is *God* who moves to choose and redeem a people for himself. The church is the result of God's sovereignty and grace (2 Tim. 1:9). It exists because God has acted graciously in history.

The fact of God's choosing a people for himself implies a distinction between those chosen and those not chosen. If God has chosen a people, then that people *really exists as a people,* a people in some sense identifiable and distinct from the world. It is not an anonymous people.

2. *The church is a pilgrim people.* Here we have an emphasis which is difficult but biblically necessary. Difficult, because it can be misconstrued to mean theological and practical with-

drawal from the world. But necessary, because without this emphasis the church tends to slip into the worst kind of worldliness.

Adam and Eve were not created to be pilgrims. God made a home for them that should have been permanent: "The LORD God planted a garden in Eden, in the east; and there he put the man whom he had formed" (Gen. 2:8). Adam and Eve were at home in the world and in harmony with their environment—morally, physically and psychologically.

But when sin entered man became a wanderer. Our first parents were expelled from the garden. After his act of murder Cain was condemned to be "a fugitive and a wanderer on the earth" (Gen. 4:12). But what happened? "Cain went away from the presence of the LORD, . . . and he built a city" (Gen. 4:16-17). The world came under the dominion of evil, and man tried to build his substitute Eden in this tainted world.[8]

So henceforth the story of redemption is the story of God's *calling out* a people for himself. This people is called to be pilgrims, to live in active tension with the world, "looking for a city not made with hands," knowing that the time of final reconciliation, the end of the pilgrimage, will come.

The church is a pilgrim people. This does not mean that it is completely divorced from, or has no responsibility for, its cultural context; the church's mission is still reconciliation. It does mean, however, a fundamental moral tension between the church and human society. The pilgrim aspect results from the estrangement produced by sin and is a reminder of and testimony to the alienation between man and his world. And this is a necessary precondition for true reconciliation.

3. *The church is a covenant people.* The relationship between God and his people is specific and is morally and ethically based. It is grounded in the covenant, and hence there exists the possibility of fidelity or infidelity to covenant provisions.

A major significance of the covenant is that it grounds God's people in real history. The covenant implies a *covenant occasion* in which the contract between God and man was actually established in space and time. The Hebrews were deeply conscious of this. Thus we have the historical giving of the law in the Old Testament and the establishing of the new covenant in the historical Last Supper, death and resurrection of Jesus Christ. The covenant is established in historical occurrences that can be recorded, commemorated and renewed.

These historical occurrences have been recorded for us in the Scriptures; hence, the Bible is the church's Book of the Covenant. The people of God is a people "under the Word." The Bible is normative for the life of the church, not because of some particular doctrine of inspiration but precisely because it *is* the Book of the Covenant.

4. *The church is a witness people.* Its task is to point to that which has happened in the past and is happening in the present which is truly the action of God. As Jess Moody reminds us, the church must be able to say "This is That"; it must have something miraculous to point to. If our only success "is that which can be explained in terms of organization and management—that is, something the world could do with the same expenditure of effort and technique, the world will one day finally repudiate us."[9]

The church must witness to God's personal acts throughout history—and, as the book of Acts makes clear, supremely to the resurrection of Jesus Christ (for example, Acts 2:32; 3:15; 4:33). It must also be able to point to the contemporary miracles of personal conversion and genuine community which give credence to the miracles of an earlier day. As John Howard Yoder emphasizes,

The political novelty which God brings into the world is a community of those who serve instead of ruling, who suffer instead of inflicting suffering, whose fellowship crosses social lines instead of reinforcing them. This new Christian community . . . is not only a vehicle of the gospel or fruit of the gospel; it is the good news.[10]

But the witnessing role is not a purely passive one. God has given the church a "ministry of reconciliation" that "through the church" God might bring about the reconciliation of "all things . . . things in heaven and things on earth" (2 Cor. 5:18; Eph. 3:10; 1:10; Col. 1:20). This gives Christians a mandate for working in various ministries of reconciliation, performing those "good works which God prepared beforehand" for the fulfilling of his plan of reconciliation (Eph. 2:10).

5. *Finally, the church is a holy people.* The biblical demand for holiness is insistent: "You shall be holy for I am holy." (See, for example, Lev. 11:44-45; 19:2; 20:7; 1 Pet. 1:15-16.) Says Paul, Christ sanctifies the church that it may be "without spot or wrinkle or any such thing, that she might be holy and without blemish" (Eph. 5:27).

This holiness is a sharing of the divine nature (2 Pet. 1:4). It is the fruit of the Spirit dwelling and acting, not only within the individual believer but within the redeemed community. It is an aspect of the fellowship of the Holy Spirit. Human personality and Christian community were made to be indwelt by the Spirit of God, and reach their potential only when they are.

Implications for Church Structure Theologically, the church is constituted the people of God, but in fact it often fails to demonstrate this reality in space and time. Whatever the so-called spiritual reasons for this lack, it must also be seen as a problem of ecclesiology, and specifically of church structure. What can the church do to incarnate this reality, to make it demonstrably visible? It seems to me that four implications are especially vital.

First, the individual believer must be able to feel himself a part of the larger corporate unity of the people of God. This means *the church must meet together in a way that encourages and expresses the fact of peoplehood.* It is meaningless to talk of peoplehood if in fact our structures stifle the experiencing of this reality.

Here again we must remember the special temporal obstacles which, in this life, believers face—obstacles which prevent our sense of peoplehood from being realized automatically. There are mystics, of course, who enjoy an isolated existence and do feel, mystically, their union with other Christians. But their experience is far from the reality of most of us, nor is it the ideal. The average Christian needs church structures which lead to a sense of peoplehood.

But what kinds of structures do build this sense of peoplehood? Obviously, structures which actually bring the people of God together at specific points in space and time. So this suggests a second guideline for church structure: *The church must meet together regularly as a large congregation.* It must actually come together as a people.

This is one reason—though not the only one—why small-group fellowships, essential as they are, are not in themselves sufficient to sustain the life of the church. The individual cells of the Body of Christ must *see* and *feel* their unity with the larger body.

It is not physically possible, of course, to bring the entire Body of Christ together at one time and place. Physical limitations require intermediate structures—whether associations, denominations, crusades or movements—which bring together a large cross section of the people of God, where the homogeneity is not social or political or economic, but spiritual.

The need for such large-group structures was brought home to me while in Brazil. In the city of São Paulo the fiery Pentecostal evangelist Manoel de Mello is building what is billed as the largest church in the world. In an already completed part of this temple thousands of his followers in the Brasil Para Cristo movement meet together each Saturday night. Packing into public buses, perhaps singing as they come, they converge on their temple. From all parts of the city and outlying areas they come, ready to share the joy and excitement of a great throng of believers. They pray, sing, witness and hear their leader. Tomorrow they will be scattered in hundreds of congregations around the city, many of which are small and struggling. But they will not be discouraged: They know they are a part of a *people* a *movement*! Something is happening, something big, something God-sized. They have seen it and felt it.

Some may scoff, speaking of "emotional release" and "crowd psychology." Certainly there are the dangers of extremes and counterfeits. But we must recognize the essential human dependence on structures which is a part of our humanity while we are bound in space and time. And one cannot deny the practical value of this identification with one's church as a people.

Actually, most new religious movements have instinctively sensed, in the beginning, the need for some form of regular large-group gatherings, whether mass rallies, evangelistic campaigns, congresses or other forms. Often mass preaching services, such as in early Methodism, fulfilled this function.

A variety of forms is possible. What is essential is the gathering together of a large group of believers, and that on a regular and frequent basis—the periodic uniting of smaller congregations and cells into a great throng.

Further, taking our cue in part from the Old Testament, we must stress the need for *covenant experiences*. Both the ancient Hebrews and the early Christians were conscious of being a people *because* something had happened. God had acted in history to choose and form a people. In the Old Testament these acts of God were periodically recalled by special festivals and celebrations. Such commemorations were covenant experiences, occasions for the remembrance and renewal of the covenant between God and man. And this suggests a third implication for church structure: *The church needs periodic festivals which have covenant significance.*

I am not talking about superficial celebrations patterned after those of the world. Rather, I mean occasions which spring from and celebrate the genuine joy and excitement of corporately sharing the fact that God has acted. This is what the Old Testament religious festivals were all about. The church needs festivals analagous to the Day of Atonement and the Feast of Tabernacles, not analagous to the Tournament of Roses, New Year's Eve or the Super Bowl.

Interestingly enough, American Protestantism used to have such a festival—the camp meeting. In the best camp meetings, whether denominational or nondenominational, the sense of peoplehood and covenant responsibility was periodically recaptured. Thousands flocked to such meetings during much of the nineteenth century.[11]

But the camp meeting has gradually faded into the mists of American folk history or been replaced by the family camp, and no suitable substitute has yet appeared. Billy Graham crusades and the rallies of the Jesus Movement have on occasion sparked some sense of peoplehood, but only sporadically and, therefore, ineffectively; their main purpose lies elsewhere.

Whatever the form of such covenant experiences, there are at least four functions they might fulfill:

1. *Celebration of the acts of God.* Reciting with joy and praise the acts of God in biblical history, in Jesus Christ (especially the incarnation, resurrection and Pentecost) and in the history of this particular subgroup of God's people.[12]

2. *Covenant renewal.* Reciting the terms of God's covenant with man, both God's part and man's part. This would of necessity involve repentance, confession and rededication to God as well as a renewed sense of fidelity to the Bible as the written Word and Book of the Covenant.

3. *Evaluation and definition.* Evaluation: Have we been faithful to the covenant? Where have we failed? What changes should be made? Have we betrayed the biblical perspective, either through pickling our faith in unbiblical traditions or through making changes that are equally unbiblical in their inspiration? And definition: What does it mean, today, to be

the people of God? What is our relationship to non-Christian culture? What are the limits of our involvement with the world?

4. *Renewal of a vision for the future.* Where there is no vision, the people perish. We must think historically and biblically about the future. We must catch a vision of future possibilities, remembering we serve a God who yet promises to do a new thing. Covenant occasions are right for the continuing definition of a biblical eschatology.

All of the foregoing brings us to a final implication of the concept of the people of God for church structure. As we have seen, the people of God does not exist for nothing or by accident. The basis of the church's existence as a people is all-important. Therefore, *in the church's structuring of itself the basis of the church's existence as a people must be kept central.*

What is this basis of the people of God? It is nothing other than the Word of God—God-in-relationship, the Person of Jesus Christ as living and active and the Bible as historically conditioned but once-for-all revealed truth (Heb. 4:12-13). The church is constituted a people by the Word of God.

Here, perhaps, is where large-group and small-group structures come together. The small group is an excellent context for Bible study and genuine theological work by the whole Body of Christ, rather than by professional theologians. Here the real biblical meaning of being the people of God in these days needs to be hammered out.

For some, it is an offense to speak of the church as a distinct people. For those who wish to emphasize the solidarity of all mankind in the face of injustice and other social ills, any suggestion that the church is or ought to be a distinct people is scandalous. But the fact remains that the Bible speaks in these terms. Further, the church as a distinct community is a practical necessity, as we have already pointed out. Truth does not exist independently of persons, and persons do not exist independently of structures of common life.

But how does one define who is and who is not a part of the people of God? What are the criteria for identification? Various solutions might be suggested, but this much is clear: The kind of structures suggested here, which heighten and define the church's sense of peoplehood, naturally tend to draw together genuine believers and repel those not sincerely interested in the things of the Spirit.

Where church structure is functional, where wineskins allow and encourage the sense of being the people of God rather than quench the Spirit, there we may hope for a new depth of Christian faithfulness and for new life in the church.

9

THE MIND OF CHRIST

The church today lives in a world increasingly hostile to all that is truly human. While there is much talk of expanded consciousness, sensitivity training, new forms of community and the like, fundamental forces are moving to undermine the uniqueness of being human. When we strip away the jargon, we often find an unvoiced conviction that, fundamentally, man is nothing more than a machine. His mind is merely "a slow-clockrate modified digital machine, with multiple distinguishable parallel processing, all working in salt water."[1]

But the church is to know the mind of Christ, the renewed image of God. In a technological age, this is revolutionary.

"We have the mind of Christ," says Paul in 1 Corinthians 2:16. And again, "Let this mind be in you, which was also in Christ Jesus" (Phil. 2:5 AV). These statements reveal two things: The character of Jesus Christ is the standard for the church, and there is a unique feature of Christ's character—what Paul here calls "mind"—which the community of God's people is to experience. And it is this very aspect of Christ's character which is most threatened in godless contemporary society. Here also we find material for new wineskins.

The Uniqueness of the Mind of Christ The characteristic word for "mind" in the New Testament is *nous*. This Greek word appears twenty-four times, twenty-one of them in Paul's writings. "Mind" in the New Testament, however, does not have the technical sense the word acquired in Greek philosophy. The New Testament usage is closer to the idea of "heart" in the Old Testament.[2] Without going into a technical study of *nous* and related words, we may say that when the New Testament speaks of mind it is referring to the totality of man as a rational, moral and spiritual being. We are confronted here with the uniqueness of man—with the image of God. We meet *personality,* and we see the relationship of such statements as "we have the mind of Christ" to declarations such as, "those whom he foreknew he also predestined to be conformed to the image of his Son" (Rom. 8:29). The Christian, restored to relationship with God through Christ in conversion, can have the mind of Christ because he was created in the image of God.

It is the image of God that makes man unique in a world of things, animals and machines. Jesus Christ, "the image of the invisible God" (Col. 1:15), came to conquer sin and restore that image. He atoned for sin and founded the church. And God's express will for the church is that "all attain to the unity of the faith and of the knowledge of the Son of God, to mature manhood, to the measure of the stature of the fulness of Christ" (Eph. 4:13). This is to incarnate the mind of Christ in the church of God.

But what is the image of God in man? What is the uniqueness of the mind of Christ? Essentially, it is the freedom to respond to God, to enter into love-community with him and, thus, with other persons. This uniqueness will naturally be seen somewhat differently in different ages and cultures. Given the context of an emerging technological society, however, I suggest the following five aspects as key elements of the mind of Christ in the church today—elements which were clearly demonstrated in the very personality and character of Jesus Christ and are thus significant for the church, his Body.

1. *Spontaneity.* Spontaneity is basic to personality. Art, love

and play all presuppose the freedom to be spontaneous—to do the unnecessary, the unplanned, the unrequired. Spontaneity is the unpredictability of Jesus, who did not quite fit anyone's mold. Spontaneity is the creative in man, the capacity and impulse to act freely. As Mildred Wynkoop observes, "The very fact of difference and unpredictability gives man his value as man."[3]

But spontaneity is the antithesis of technique. Therefore, spontaneity is not permitted in the world of technology—it is too dangerous. The worst sin of a machine or a computer is to be unpredictable.

Predictability is understandable when we are dealing with machines. But today the complexity of modern society requires the increasing use of machines to regulate human behavior. And this is accompanied by the growth of effective means for controlling society through a technology of human behavior. Futurologists Kahn and Wiener write,

The modern industrial society is highly differentiated and therefore requires great integration in order to function. . . .

Greater wealth and improved technology give us a wider range of alternatives; but once an alternative has been chosen, much regulation and imposed order is needed. Thus with geometric increase in the complexity and organization of modern life, corresponding . . . increases in the scope and complexity of human and organization controls will become necessary. One need not assume the triumph of the police mentality . . . to foresee this. Each restriction will have its valid and attractive rationale, which may even be libertarian.[4]

In other words, the more complicated society becomes, the more man must be regulated. "No Parking" signs were not necessary before cars, and pollution controls were not needed before the Industrial Revolution.

In technological society, spontaneity may become the true test of freedom—spontaneity, not in the sense of a "freedom" to turn inward to a self-indulgent irrationalism (which is no real freedom and produces no effective action in the world), but the freedom to create, to act, to love in ways that produce and change human relationships and social structures. It is this spontaneity, unique to human personality and enabled by the Holy Spirit, which is threatened by technological society.

2. *Individuality.* Each human being is a unique individual. He has value because he is created and loved by God. Therefore something unquantifiable is found in man. Human beings can be quantified, but only at the loss of what is most uniquely human.

Since man was created in God's image he has value *because he is,* regardless of what he can do. If man does not share the uniqueness of God's infinity, he most certainly shares the dimension of personality—to borrow a thought from Francis Schaeffer.

Technological society, of course, is not ultimately interested in what is unique in each individual but rather in what is identical—what can be counted, standardized, computerized. And the increasing sophistication of behavioral technology greatly broadens the range of the quantifiable. Already more advanced technological societies have moved far beyond the mere quantification of income, education, employment, residence, credit standing and the like, and are moving into records of religious beliefs, political preferences, mental health and personality types. Some are even seeking a *quantifiable* index to the *quality* of life.

Alvin Toffler argues that advanced technology tends toward diversification rather than standardization.[5] This may well be where technology eventually leads, but such diversification is not an unmixed blessing. Technology gradually reaches such a sophisticated level that it is able to subdivide people according to increasingly limited criteria, with the end in view of attaining a particular result. It is superficial therefore to equate technological diversity with greater human freedom, as Toffler tends to do. Rather, diversification facilitates manipulation. This is, in fact, the goal, though it is seldom stated so baldly.

All manipulation is a threat to true individuality—and hence to true spirituality. In the church, manipulation produces a synthetic religion in which religious "experience" is technically induced and maintained. The believer becomes object, not subject; an "it," not an "I." We need a healthy fear today of any tendency to reduce evangelism and religious experience to mere technology.

Because Jesus Christ died for each person, and not just for "humanity," and because he saw worth in each person and treated him so, the Christian church must never lose the biblical emphasis on individuality. In the face of the quantification of society and the manipulation of man, a Christian must insist that individuality is a gift from God and an integral part of the mind of Christ.

3. *Moral sense.* Even without the light of the Bible, man distinguishes between right and wrong, good and evil. This moral awareness is a dimension of the image of God in man. Through the Scriptures we understand that the question is not, however, fundamentally one of right and wrong, not a matter of morality and moral codes. Essentially, man's moral sense is his awareness that he is a responsible being before the Creator-God. God exists and creates; therefore man, created in the divine image, is responsible and response-able before him, and in this relationship of responsibility man finds the meaning of his life.

But what happens to morality in a technological society? Two things. First, there is a blunting of the moral sense through the eclipse of ultimate meaning. Industrialization and urbanization break down traditional worldviews with their accompanying mores and place society in flux. A general wave of "immorality" and the "breakdown of moral standards" follows. When this occurs in a society heavily influenced by the Christian faith, the result is a general rejection of traditional Christian morality and an actualization of the kind of moral degeneration now evident in the United States and Western Europe.

But man cannot live long in a moral vacuum; he must have a morality. And technology expands to fill the vacuum, for technology brings its own morality. Technology is concerned with means, not ultimately with ends. What is technologically feasible (the means) is good in itself, and the question of ends becomes superfluous. Though some voices question the identification of technology with progress, the march of technology itself is able, in the long run, to quiet these protests. Technological progress is good in itself (better automobiles and television sets, better detergents and cleaners, more space exploration). And even when techniques are perceived as not necessarily good, man discovers they are essential for survival (antipollution controls, the pill, new techniques of surveillance, better bombs, computerized information banks and so on). And how can what is essential for survival be doubted?

Thus technology produces its own moral values—what Jacques Ellul calls "technological morality." This new morality, says Ellul, "tends to bring human behavior into harmony with the technological world, to set up a new scale of values in terms of technology, and to create new virtues."[6] Technology itself will provide the means for instilling such a morality and winning adherence to it. For, says Ellul,

> ... *the techniques of psychology will be able to reach into* [*the*] *heart itself, to personalize the objective reasons for the behavior, to obtain through technical procedures loyalty and good will, joy itself in the carrying out of the "duty," which like everything else ceases to be painful and exhausting in the comfortable world of techniques.*[7]

B. F. Skinner has already shown the way to such an induced morality by arguing that morality is, after all, no more than "a problem in human behavior." How people feel morally, therefore, says Skinner, "is a question for which a science of behavior should have an answer."[8] Behavioral technology will, when called upon, fabricate a morality conducive to social needs.

Such a technological morality is antithetical to the Christian faith, not because the specific behavior induced would be "immoral"—it might, in fact, be highly commendable—but because it is a morality of means, not of ends; of technological necessity, not of personal relationships between man and man and between man and God. It is a morality on the level of things and nonconscious being, not on the high level of conscious persons. The social behavior of ants may be quite decorous, but it is not for that reason an adequate model for human morality.

The church, however, is called upon to deepen man's moral capacity and give it meaning through Christ-centered relationships, both horizontal and vertical. The church is in danger of an insidious worldliness at this point. For all its professed interest in persons, too often the institutional church betrays itself in the way it actually treats people. Man's moral sense—given as a capacitator for true, loving and holy relationships—can all too easily be manipulated by "spiritual" techniques used to keep people in line. A warning to a small child to be quiet in church because he is in God's house, besides being theologically suspect, can be simply a technique to induce certain desired behavior. And that is only one small example of what often happens on a much larger scale.

4. *Self-consciousness.* Man, as Francis Schaeffer has noted, "is distinguished as man by the fact that in a very real way he lives inside his own head."[9] The Psalms repeatedly speak of this interior life of man—that life which only the individual knows and whose depths go deeper than our own consciousness and are known only to God. This reflects the image of God in man and is essential to the formation of the mind of Christ in a believer.

There is much in the world that can either develop, distort or deaden self-consciousness. Much that comes through television and films actually has such a deadening effect, as do alcohol and many kinds of drugs. Most forms of Eastern mysticism tend in the same direction: the swallowing up of one's own self-consciousness in a transpersonal, universal Whole. In George Orwell's *1984* the development of "Newspeak" was actually intended to limit consciousness and eliminate conscious choices, and thus reduce behavior from a rational to an instinctual level: "Orthodoxy is unconsciousness."[10]

In a world which tends to reduce man's self-awareness, or to treat it as a mere evolutionary quirk legitimately subject to behavioral engineering, the church of Jesus Christ must never forget that self-consciousness is a gift from God. Therefore it should be affirmed, not as the basis for a morbid spiritual introspection but as the indispensable foundation for communication, for love, for volition, and hence for worship. Self-consciousness is essential for true freedom.

5. *Volition.* The Bible speaks constantly of the will of God, and Jesus said, "I have come . . . not to do my own will, but the will of him who sent me" (Jn. 6:38). Volition is part of the image of God and of the mind of Christ.

Much contemporary psychology (as well as so-called secular theology, when we examine its presuppositions) denies the possibility of true volition. Man behaves in a certain way, but the belief that this behavior springs from a conscious choice is an illusion. Beginning with a purely empirical presupposition, this is the only conclusion one can logically reach. Volition, purpose, intention—all are beyond the possibility of scientific investigation and therefore presumed not to be real.

By contrast, a Christian begins with the fact of the revealed Word of God, and thus with a personal, volitional, conscious God rather than the blindered view of an empirical presupposition. The Christian faith is unthinkable without the fact of the *will* of God—and, derivatively, the will of man.

The mind of Christ does not turn a Christian into an automaton of the Holy Spirit. The goal is not to be "controlled" by the Spirit. Rather, through the presence of the Spirit, a Christian is enabled to freely exercise his will to do God's will. Christians, of all men, should be "willful," but with their will bowed before God, as the creature before the Creator.

The church should give due emphasis to this fact of volition, especially when society either manipulates or preempts man's will. In emerging postindustrial society man either finds his range of *significant* choices increasingly limited or else he confronts *overchoice,* a dizzying multiplication of choices which tends to incapacitate him.[11] One can choose, for instance, between dozens of insignificant options on a car—colors, styles, accessories, horsepower and so on—but not between a gasoline and an electric engine, a far more significant choice.

Equally important is the whole area of advertising and propaganda. John Kenneth Galbraith writes of the "massive growth in the apparatus of persuasion and exhortation that is associated with the sale of goods." The average man (better known as "consumer") is the target of incessant propaganda about how he should use his money. "On no other matter, religious, political, or moral, is he so elaborately instructed," observes Galbraith.[12]

But politics is not far behind industry. The 1968 and 1972 U.S. presidential campaigns witnessed propaganda efforts unprecedented in extent, expense and sophistication. On the Republican side, the Watergate affair (as has now been made painfully evident) was no mere aberration but was part of an overall coordinated campaign of political persuasion (one might say manipulation)—a campaign in which even the FBI was used as a political instrument. Computers identified those sectors of the electorate most susceptible to Republican persuasion so that unnecessary effort and expense would not be wasted on unresponsive groups. Similar techniques will likely be repeated in the future with increasing effectiveness and discretion, regardless of party labels.

This vast network of persuasion, involving industry, government, education and perhaps even religion, is one of the features of postindustrial society. The trend is toward both the limitation and manipulation of significant choices.

What does this mean for the church? The church faces an increasingly difficult task in imitating the mind of Christ. It will be tempted to rely on secular propaganda techniques to win converts and produce "Christian" behavior rather than taking the harder but deeper road of true spiritual growth-toward-maturity through the recovery of the biblical meaning of the church.

Implications for Church Structure What does all this mean for wineskins? How should the church be structured today so that her members may resist the pulls and pressures of contemporary society? How may Christians have the mind of Christ?

The church must be structured so as to affirm the uniqueness and value of human personality. It must insist that what is true of individual human persons is equally true of the church: It has value because it is the work of God. Many today would reduce the church to a technique, a means to an end, and say therefore that the church exists not for itself but to serve. But this is only a half-truth. The church is the Body of Christ. Christ died for the church and loves the church, and therefore the church has worth. Regardless of what it does in the world, the church has value and meaning because God created it. This is really another way of saying, after all, that salvation is "by grace, through faith," and "not by works." And yet the church is "created in Christ Jesus *for* good works," that it "should walk in them" (Eph. 2:8-10).

More specifically, we may identify the following implications for church structure:

Church structure must make room for the individual if the mind of Christ is to become a reality in the church. The whole sphere of the personal must be the special domain of the church.

This may sound strange, since the legitimate point has often been made that Western Christianity has tended to *over*-emphasize the individual. But the biblical corrective is not to ride a pendulum swing to the other extreme; neither is it to seek a bland, middle-of-the-road approach. Rather, the solution is to affirm the breadth of the revealed Word of God: The gospel has both corporate and individual dimensions, and both must be incarnated in the church. So any unbiblical swing away from persons as individuals must be resisted.

Look at Jesus Christ, whose mind is to be in us. His life showed his solidarity with all mankind. He died for all. But his uniqueness as an individual person stands out clearly, not solely because he was the unique incarnation of the invisible God but because of the very individuality of his humanness. Jesus was not the incarnation of some generalized humanity; he was and is a particular, individual person.

Church structure must be compatible with this individual emphasis. Structures should bring persons face-to-face with Jesus Christ as responsible individuals. Christian education and training must focus on the individual and not allow him to be lost in the group, even while using group dynamics and interaction. In every area of the church's life there must be a recognition that Christ calls, saves and inhabits individual persons for his glory, and that his work will show itself in ways as varied as crystals of snow or leaves on a tree—as varied as human personality itself.

Obviously, this need will require a proper emphasis on one-to-one relationships in the Christian community. This should be not primarily in the traditional sense of pastor-to-member, but in the sense of a whole glorious web of believer-to-believer relationships which become the hidden structure of community. Here again, small groups are necessary to provide opportunity and stimulus for such relationships.

An implication here which I can only mention in passing is

the importance of marriage and the family for the church. These are the basic personality-forming institutions God has given us, and they must function hand-in-hand with the church. In a sense, the Christian home *is* one of the structures of the church. A great need today is to rethink the family on the basis of the biblical understanding of the Body of Christ.

A person in need never got lost in the crowd when Jesus passed by. This is a parable for church structure today.

Second, *church structure must be flexible and varied.* This is the meaning of spontaneity and self-consciousness, discussed above. Church structure must provide a variety of outlets for ministry and for expressing the meaning of faith in Christ. There must be some freedom of choice in discovering and developing a Christian lifestyle (or a variety of Christian lifestyles) for our age, but within the authority of Scripture and the context of Christian community.

The life of the Christian community should produce the kinds of changes suggested in the following example:

In the past couple of years I have had fellowship with several brothers who once served with a Christian organization whose goal was world evangelization. The zeal within this organization had led to a rule that each staff member must witness a certain number of times per week. Reports had to be filed on this by each one. Finally God began to speak to these particular men about what He wanted in their lives. Not long after leaving this organization, one of these men said to me, "It's really great! I'm just beginning to learn to live. I'm discovering what it really means just to be free to be like Christ." . . .

Another of these fellows shared with me one day the exciting discovery that he had made. He had found that he didn't have to go around with secret cravings lurking beneath the surface all the time. He had found that the resurrection life of Jesus was able to lift him above the problem by replacing it with a wholesome love from God for others. He was free![13]

Structure must be flexible. In those areas where no revealed pattern has been given, changes should be made as circumstances and biblical fidelity warrant. Such areas include time, place and frequency of meetings, organization for specific ministries, and most aspects of church government. Here flexibility, not just tradition, should rule. The very silence of the Bible concerning specific structures should alert us to their subsidiary and culturally bound nature and remind us that constant re-evaluation in the light of the Word of God is necessary if the mind of Christ is going to become a reality.

To do the work of God in the world the church is naturally forced to adopt structural patterns (organizations, institutions and so on) which are appropriate to the surrounding culture.[14] But such structures should always be understood as not being the essence of the church, and therefore as subject to revision, adaptation or even dissolution. In recent years considerable sociological research has been done about flexible, short-term or "self-destruct" organizational forms. The institutional church could benefit greatly from such studies. Their application might be useful in areas where the church's structure is organizational in nature, including, especially, denominational structures.

Third, *church structure must help sustain a Christian's life in the world.* The church's task is not to keep Christians off the streets but to send them out equipped for kingdom tasks. The Christian community must be structured for such equipping. The more society becomes hostile to Christian values, the more a Christian will depend for his very life on living, supportive structures of community.

Such structures must reinforce the values of personality through small groups, a new emphasis on the family and other one-to-one relationships. This may require forming special-interest cells for Christians called to specific ministries in the world. And certainly it will mean a serious theological involvement with the Scriptures to determine the shape of Christian responsibility in society.

A final implication comes in here: *Church structure must be built upon spiritual gifts.* The gifts of the Spirit testify implicitly to the diversity of human personality. Paul emphasizes in 1 Corinthians 12—14, Ephesians 4 and elsewhere that the essential function of spiritual gifts is to build up the Christian community. This is synonymous with incarnating the mind of Christ in the church. Spiritual gifts form one of the basic foundations for a proper understanding of the church.

Individual Christians—and therefore the whole community of faith—experience the mind of Christ only as God-given spiritual gifts are awakened and exercised. No Christian with an atrophied gift will easily come to demonstrate the mind of Christ. Further, the dynamic interaction of gifts within the community is necessary for achieving the mind of Christ corporately. We understand this on the basis of the figure of the body: The ear hears, not because it enjoys hearing, but that the body may function. The hand grasps, not just because it needs the exercise (which it does!), but that the body may act.

An emphasis on spiritual gifts means church structure which is dynamic, interactive and organic. It means a conscious resistance to secular organizational models for the church as community. The structure of the community must be based on biblical models and figures, not on models taken from secular industry, education and government. In many cases a proper emphasis on spiritual gifts means a fundamental rethinking of church structure.

A certain tension, even antithesis, must prevail between the church and society. This tension is biblical, in the spirit of John 17:14-16 and similar passages, and will become more pronounced throughout the world in coming decades. The unique value of the mind of Christ will be denied by society in general, and therefore will become pivotal for the church.

But this is no argument for total withdrawal from the world, for building monasteries of the spirit. Nor is it to deny that Jesus Christ is lord of all creation, that he has "disarmed the principalities and powers and made a public example of them, triumphing over them" (Col. 2:15). God's plan is still "to unite all things in him, things in heaven and things on earth" (Eph. 1:10). The church shares with Christ the secret that the present battle will be won by Christ, for the victory has already been won on the cross. In the face of a godless society a Christian has confidence to work in the world, raising signs of the kingdom which, by faith, he sees coming.

To incarnate the mind of Christ in the church requires some clear thinking and some rethinking of the whole matter of spiritual gifts, beyond what has already been said in this chapter. I will now deal with this matter in more detail.

10

THE PLACE OF SPIRITUAL GIFTS

God creates. Hence man, created in the divine image, is also creative. And the Spirit of God who was "moving over the face of the waters" at the dawn of creation is the same Spirit who, according to Scripture, operates in the church, giving to each Christian "the manifestation of the Spirit for the common good" (1 Cor. 12:7).

The Christian faith makes room for gifts and creativity on the basis of the important biblical doctrine of the gifts of the Spirit. And yet, great confusion exists regarding spiritual gifts. Too often specific Christian traditions—implicitly, if not explicitly—deny the possibility of real creativity. The institutional church often shows a serious and crippling misunderstanding of the biblical concept of spiritual gifts. And even though there is a great renewal of interest in the gifts of the Spirit today, this interest has often generated more heat than light.

One cannot really understand what the New Testament means when it speaks of the church unless one understands what it teaches about the gifts of the Spirit. Spiritual gifts are primarily a matter not of individual Christian experience but of the corporate life of the church. Gifts are given for, and in the context of, community.

I have already suggested in chapter 6 how our misunderstanding of spiritual gifts affects our concept of the pastoral ministry and feeds the "Superstar" idea, and in the last chapter we noted that structure must be compatible with gifts. We need now to discuss more positively, and in somewhat more detail, the place of spiritual gifts in the life of the church.

The contemporary church in its institutional form makes little room for spontaneous spiritual gifts. Worse yet, too often it does not need spiritual gifts in order to function more or less successfully. When the local church is structured after an institutional rather than a charismatic model, spiritual gifts are replaced by aptitude, education and technique, and thus become superfluous.

Several common misunderstandings of spiritual gifts today need to be corrected and shown for what they are: unbiblical tendencies that effectively quench the working of the Holy Spirit in the Christian community. I suggest, in particular, five such tendencies.

1. *The tendency to deny or discredit spiritual gifts.* In its most extreme form, this tendency says the gifts of the Spirit were given as miraculous signs at Pentecost but have no legitimacy today. Gifts of healing, prophecy and tongues are no longer considered valid. In a milder form this tendency admits, in theory, the validity of spiritual gifts but in practice is suspicious of them and tends to discredit them. All spiritual gifts, and especially the more controversial ones, are thought to be superfluous at best and heretical at worst.

Such a position, however, arbitrarily limits the operation of the Holy Spirit and the applicability of the New Testament to our day. There is no more warrant, for instance, for applying chapters 12 and 14 of 1 Corinthians exclusively to the early church than there is for limiting the thirteenth chapter in this way. Gifts and love go together—in the twentieth century as in the first.

The denial of spiritual gifts really indicates a basic misunderstanding of the nature of such gifts. Those who fear spiritual gifts (and often the problem is, in reality, one of fear) usually conceive of such gifts as highly individualistic, irrational and eccentric manifestations that disturb the unity of the Body of Christ. But such a caricature is not at all what the Bible means by the gifts of the Spirit.

Spiritual gifts cannot be depreciated without a corresponding devaluation of the biblical understanding of the church and the Spirit-filled life. The *charismata* are not something artificially tacked on; neither are they temporally or culturally bound. They are cross-culturally valid, and it is their presence in the church which makes the church cross-culturally relevant. It is no accident that Paul, both in Romans 12 and Ephesians 4, relates the unity of the Spirit's ministry in the church to the diversity of gifts. The appeal to "present your bodies as a living sacrifice" and "be transformed by the renewal of your mind" is followed by the appeal, "Having gifts that differ according to the grace given us, let us use them" (Rom. 12:1-6). Both injunctions are for today.

We simply have no authority to declare specific gifts invalid. It may be difficult to accept the full range of biblical teaching here, but this is necessary to avoid impoverishing the church. And it is absolutely essential for a truly biblical doctrine of the church and its ministry.

2. *The tendency to over-individualize spiritual gifts.* Western Christianity in general has tended to over-individualize the gospel to the detriment of the gospel's communal and collective aspects,[1] and contemporary conceptions of spiritual gifts have suffered from this tendency. Thus spiritual gifts are too often thought of as strictly a matter of an individual's "private" relationship to God, without regard for the Christian community. In contrast to this, Paul repeatedly emphasizes that the Spirit's gifts are for the edification of the church and lose their significance if this emphasis is lost. The general principle is, "To each is given the manifestation of the Spirit *for the common good*" (1 Cor. 12:7). The individual gift is balanced by community responsibility and interaction. Paul prefaces his

comments on gifts in Romans 12 with the words, "We, though many, are one body in Christ, and individually members one of another" (Rom. 12:5). This is the biblical balance, and spiritual gifts can rightly be understood only in this context.

The biblical conception is that the community of believers acts as the controlling context for the exercise of gifts, thus discouraging individualistic aberrations. And gifts *must* operate in this way. The church is, to use Gordon Cosby's phrase, "a gift-evoking, gift-bearing community." And when the church really functions in this way, the various gifts not only reinforce each other, they also act as check-and-balance to prevent extremes. Here the New Testament analogy of the body is helpful. The hand or foot is prevented from some extreme action by its connection to the body's various organs and systems. Functioning as part of the body, the hand is helpful and nearly indispensable, but cut off from the body it becomes grotesque and useless. So it is with spiritual gifts.

It is at this point, incidentally, that small Bible study groups find their utility. The small Spirit-led group builds community and provides the context for both awakening spiritual gifts and disciplining their use. As a consequence of many such cells, the whole larger community of the church is edified.

Spiritual gifts are given not merely for personal enjoyment nor even primarily for an individual's own spiritual growth, although this, too, is important. Gifts are given for the common good, "that the church may be edified" (1 Cor. 14:5).

3. *The tendency to confuse spiritual gifts and native abilities.* The error here lies in the tendency to go to one extreme or the other: to make spiritual gifts and native abilities either synonymous or else antithetical.

Each person is born with latent potentialities which should be developed and employed to the glory of God. This is stewardship. But when the New Testament speaks of spiritual gifts, it goes beyond this. Paul says the Holy Spirit "apportions to each one individually as he wills" (1 Cor. 12:11). This suggests a direct, immediate relationship between God and man through conversion and life in the Spirit. The gifts of the Spirit result from the operation of the Spirit in the life of a believer, and so are something more than merely the wise and faithful use of native abilities. Gifts must be understood as, literally, *gifts* of the *Spirit.*

But how and when does the Spirit operate? Only after conversion? The Holy Spirit is the Spirit of creation that was "moving over the face of the waters," the same Spirit who said to Jeremiah, "Before I formed you in the womb I knew you, and before you were born I consecrated you; I appointed you a prophet to the nations" (Jer. 1:5). God is sovereign and omniscient, and we must not suppose that he begins to work in a person's life only after conversion. There really is no such thing as a "native" ability; "What have you that you did not receive?" (1 Cor. 4:7). It is not too much to say that God in his foreknowledge has given to each individual at birth those talents that he later wills to awaken and ignite. A spiritual gift is often a God-given ability that has caught fire.

A native capacity does not really become a gift of the Spirit until it is given over to the Spirit and used by him. The principle of crucifixion and resurrection, of dying and rising, applies here. Natural abilities remain in the plane of powerless human works until given to God in self-sacrifice.

In his perceptive discussion of spiritual gifts in *Full Circle,* David R. Mains writes,

In those areas where I have natural abilities, such as a facility for public speaking, the difference between their being talents or gifts of the Holy Spirit is found in my attitude. If I recognize the talent as from God, and in prayer and continual dedication commit it to Him to be used in ministry in a special way, it becomes a gift of the Holy Spirit with supernatural expression. The proof of this is seen in the gradual way God increases the gift for His service.[2]

So talents and gifts are neither synonymous nor antithetical. Both, after all, are bestowed by God. It is no accident that converted salesmen often make good evangelists. God is not capricious. Although we must not limit the sovereign working of the Spirit, yet we may normally expect some correspondence between a person's native abilities and personality traits—latent or developed—and the spiritual gifts God will bring forth in him. The Spirit intends to transform us into what we were meant to become, not into Xerox copies of each other.

4. *The tendency to exaggerate some gifts and depreciate others.* This is one of the most serious and most common distortions of spiritual gifts—the tendency to restrict legitimate gifts to only certain specific ones. How serious this aberration has become is seen in the fact that any discussion of spiritual gifts today usually becomes sidetracked on the question of tongues. The tendency to think of spiritual gifts only in terms of the more spectacular gifts such as tongues, healing or prophecy is an aberration which must be avoided. All gifts are important, all gifts are necessary and all are given by God for the common good.

An examination of the relevant biblical passages suggests that the various gifts mentioned are intended as representative, not exhaustive. The multiform operation of the Spirit may awaken an infinity of gifts; gifts may be as varied as human personality. The New Testament lists the specific leadership gifts of apostle, prophet, evangelist and pastor-teacher (Eph. 4:11; 1 Cor. 12:28). But such designations as utterance of knowledge, helps, service, acts of mercy and so forth, may be understood as general categories which include a wide spectrum of specific gifts and ministries. Thus any ability ignited and used by the Holy Spirit—whether in music, art, writing, intercessory prayer, homemaking, hospitality, listening or whatever—is a legitimate spiritual gift. If God has given the gift, then it is good and is intended to be used. The biblical teaching is plain: "As each has received a gift, employ it for one another, as good stewards of God's varied grace: . . . in order that in everything God may be glorified through Jesus

Christ" (1 Pet. 4:10-11).

The problem, too often, is the failure to affirm the full range of gifts—the failure to appreciate "God's varied grace." The fact is that all gifts are important, and none is an anomaly when exercised rightly in the context of community. Thus it is as wrong to overemphasize preaching and teaching and to deny tongues and healing as it is, on the contrary, so to emphasize the more spectacular gifts that the more mundane gifts are lost sight of. The Holy Spirit acts so "that there may be no discord in the body" only when all gifts are affirmed and operate cooperatively. To quote David Mains again,

Every true member of the local church has a minimum of one gift, and most people have many. Since no one has every gift, and everyone has at least one, there exists an interdependence among the members of the church. Scripture teaches (1 Cor. 12:22-25) that the less spectacular gifts are more necessary than the showy ones. In other words, the church can go a long time without a miracle, but let it try to exist without acts of mercy or contributions! . . . How disabled the body of Christ has become because our primary purpose for church attendance has been to hear one man exercise his gifts, rather than to prepare all the people to develop their gifts for ministry, not only within the church but also to society.[3]

The function of a local church should be to expect, identify and awaken the varied gifts that sleep within the community of believers. When all gifts are affirmed under the leadership of the Holy Spirit and in the context of mutual love, each gift is important and no gift becomes an aberration. Whether the Holy Spirit chooses to grant to a particular local congregation all the gifts mentioned in Scripture remains, of course, a divine option. We have nothing to say about that, for the Holy Spirit is sovereign. We can be sure, however, that God will give to each local church all the gifts really necessary for its own upbuilding in love.

5. *The tendency to divorce spiritual gifts from the cross.* This tendency arises from the failure to incarnate the tension between

the cross and the *charismata,* between Passover and Pentecost. It is the tendency, on the one hand, to emphasize gifts in such a way that the cross is lost sight of and the community is fractured by self-centeredness, or, just the opposite, to deny any emphasis on gifts because of this tendency toward self-centeredness and self-aggrandizement.

What is the biblical position? How can the fact of each person's discovering and exercising his gifts be reconciled with Christ's fundamental words, "If any man would come after me, let him deny himself and take up his cross and follow me" (Mk. 8:34)?

There *is* a danger here, for spiritual gifts are often misunderstood. The New Testament teaching about spiritual gifts is not a call for each Christian to "do his own thing" and forget the welfare of the group and the need of the world. Ministry is not determined exclusively by personal desire, but by the cross.

And yet, biblically, there is no contradiction between gift-affirmation and self-denial. In fact, the two go together. The biblical principle, again, is that of death and resurrection. As one is crucified with Christ and dies to his own will, the Holy Spirit resurrects within him his significant gift. So the spiritual gift, rightly exercised, is not self-centeredness; it is self-giving.

But we must go further than this, and say that *a Christian discovers the true meaning of the crucifixion as he really begins to exercise his gift.* Faithful ministry of the gift of the Spirit will lead him into depths of self-giving he never dreamed possible —and God planned it that way. This is the way we are created —psychologically, emotionally and spiritually.

Here we find the meaning of the life and death of Jesus Christ, God's Son and the perfect man. We may suppose that Jesus possessed, at least potentially, all the gifts of the Spirit, and he publicly exercised many of them—apostle, evangelist, healer, prophet, teacher, helper, comforter, friend. And the faithful exercise of his ministry led him not to the throne, but to the cross. But it led beyond as well—to resurrection.

"For to this you have been called, because Christ also suffered for you, leaving you an example, that you should follow in his steps" (1 Pet. 2:21). *Here* we find the meaning of the gifts of the Spirit.

Elizabeth O'Connor has written insightfully along this line in her book, *Eighth Day of Creation.* "When one really becomes practical about gifts, they spell out responsibility and sacrifice," she says, Further,

The identifying of gifts brings to the fore . . . the issue of commitment. Somehow if I name my gift and it is confirmed, I cannot "hang loose" in the same way. I would much rather be committed to God in the abstract than be committed to him at the point of my gifts. . . . Doors will close on a million lovely possibilities. I will become a painter or a doctor only if denial becomes a part of my picture of reality. Commitment at the point of my gifts means that I must give up being a straddler. Somewhere in the deeps of me I know this. Life will not be the smorgasbord I have made it, sampling and tasting here and there. My commitment will give me an identity.[4]

Spiritual gifts come to their full biblical legitimacy and meaning only in the rhythm of incarnation-crucifixion-resurrection.

Great confusion exists today about spiritual gifts. And yet the biblical teaching is clear, if we seek it. The various distinctions I have suggested here are merely attempts to peel away layers of culturally defined conceptions so that the biblical teachings can be seen.

The urgent need today is that spiritual gifts be seen and understood in the context of ecclesiology, as in the New Testament. A biblical understanding of spiritual gifts is absolutely essential for a biblical conception of the church. For this will determine whether our ecclesiology is based on a charismatic or an institutional model.

When spiritual gifts are misunderstood—through being over-individualized, denied, divorced from community or otherwise distorted—it is the church which suffers. The church truly becomes the church only when the biblical meaning of spiritual gifts is recovered. A church whose life and ministry is not built upon the exercise of spiritual gifts is, biblically, a contradiction in terms.

In the last several years the Holy Spirit himself has seemingly been calling his church back to the reality of spiritual gifts. Local churches have been renewed, books have been written and a gradual gift-consciousness has developed.

Three local churches which, in widely differing ways, have discovered the practical reality of spiritual gifts form the background for three helpful books which deal in part with gifts: *Body Life* by Ray C. Stedman, *Full Circle* by David R. Mains (to which I have already referred) and *Brethren, Hang Loose!* by Robert Girard.[5] All three books are helpful, and *Body Life*, in particular, gives a highly practical biblical exposition of the various gifts and suggestions on how to identify them.

From the perspective of missions and missionary strategy, C. Peter Wagner has also been emphasizing the importance of discovering and using spiritual gifts. I would particularly recommend his *Frontiers in Missionary Strategy* and *Stop the World, I Want to Get On.*[6]

There is no teaching more practical than that about the gifts of the Spirit. The discovery of his spiritual gift often turns a frustrated, guilt-ridden Christian into a happy and effective disciple. In my own case, the discovery of gifts has clarified the ministry to which God has called me and opened new vistas of service. When I identified and named my spiritual gifts, it seemed as if all the contradictory pieces of my life suddenly fell into place. I found the key to what God was doing in and through my life.

Happy, effective service should be the result of identifying and coming to terms with the gifts the Spirit has given us. For it is Christ himself who "gives gifts to men" in order that they may happily glorify him.

11
THE SMALL GROUP AS BASIC STRUCTURE

A small group of eight to twelve people meeting together informally in homes is the most effective structure for the communication of the gospel in modern seculurban society. Such groups are better suited to the mission of the church in today's urban world than are traditional church services, institutional church programs or the mass communication media. Methodologically speaking, the small group offers the best hope for the discovery and use of spiritual gifts and for renewal within the church.

This is one of the principal conclusions suggested by the analysis in the previous chapters. I argue for the small group as the basic church structure not primarily because its usefulness has been abundantly demonstrated in recent years through the proliferation of neighborhood Bible studies and various kinds of sharing and *koinonia* groups, although this in itself is highly significant. My argument springs, rather, from the inherent possibilities of the small group and its essential compatibility with the nature of the church, biblically understood.

The small group was the basic unit of the church's life during its first two centuries. There were no church buildings then; Christians met almost exclusively in private homes (and seldom, as we often think, in the catacombs). In fact, the use of small groups of one kind or another seems to be a common element in all significant movements of the Holy Spirit throughout church history. Early Pietism was nurtured by the *collegio pietatis,* or house meetings for prayer, Bible study and discussion.[1] The small group was a basic aspect of the Wesleyan Revival in England, with the proliferation of John Wesley's "class meetings." Small groups undergirded the Holiness Revival that swept America in the late 1800s and led, in part, to the modern Pentecostal movement.[2] More significantly, the road to the Reformation was paved by small-group Bible studies.[3] If nothing more, these facts surely suggest that small groups are conducive to the reviving ministry of the Holy Spirit.

Today the church needs to rediscover what the early Christians found: That small group meetings are something essential to Christian experience and growth. That the success of a church function is not measured by body count. That without the small group the church in urban society simply does not experience one of the most basic essentials of the gospel—true, rich, deep Christian soul-fellowship, or *koinonia.*

Advantages of Small Group Structure The small group offers a number of advantages over other forms of the church in an urban world:

1. *It is flexible.* Because the group is small, it can easily change its procedure or functions to meet changing situations or to accomplish different objectives. Because of its informality it has little need for rigid patterns of operation. It is free to be flexible as to the place, time, frequency and length of its meetings. It can easily disband when it has fulfilled its purpose without upsetting the institutional seismograph. These things can be said of virtually no other aspect of most church programming.

2. *It is mobile.* A small group may meet in a home, office, shop or nearly any other place. It is not bound to that building on the corner of First and Elm that we call "church." It can go

where the people are (or where the action is) and does not have to rely on persuading strangers to enter a foreign environment.

3. *It is inclusive.* A small group can demonstrate a winsome openness to people of all kinds. As Elton Trueblood says,

When a person is drawn into a little circle, devoted to prayer and to deep sharing of spiritual resources, he is well aware that he is welcomed for his own sake, since the small group has no budget, no officers concerned with the success of their administration, and nothing to promote.[4]

A small group provides the context in which a person can be seen, as Oswald Chambers put it, "as a fact, not as an illustration of a prejudice." Thus it holds some hope for overcoming social and racial barriers.

4. *It is personal.* Christian communication suffers from impersonality. Often it is too slick, too professional, and therefore too impersonal. But in a small group person meets person; communication takes place at the personal level. This is why, contradictory as it may seem, a small group may really reach more people than the mass communication media. The mass media reach millions superficially but few profoundly. The church should use all available forms of communication, but in proclaiming a personal Christ nothing can substitute for personal communication.

5. *It can grow by division.* A small group is effective only while small, but it can easily reproduce itself. It can multiply like living cells into two, four, eight or more, depending on the vitality of each group. There are endless possibilities for numerical growth without correspondingly large financial outlays or spiritual impact dilution.

6. *It can be an effective means of evangelism.* The evangelism which will be most effective in the city will use small groups as its basic methodology. It will find the small group provides the best environment in which sinners can hear the convicting, winning voice of the Holy Spirit and come alive spiritually

through faith. It will find that faith is contagious when fellowship is genuine. Robert Raines testifies in *New Life in the Church,*

I have watched proportionately more lives genuinely converted in and through small group meetings for prayer, Bible study, and the sharing of life than in the usual organizations and activities of the institutional church.[5]

7. *It requires a minimum of professional leadership.* Many church members who could never direct a choir, preach a sermon, lead a youth group or do house-to-house visitation can lead a small group Bible study. Competent leadership is needed in such groups, but experience has shown that such leaders can be developed in the average church through one to two key initial groups. A staff of trained professionals is not required.

8. *It is adaptable to the institutional church.* The small group does not require throwing out the organized church. Small groups can be introduced without by-passing or undercutting the church, although the serious incorporation of small groups into the overall ministry of the church requires some adjustments and is bound to eventually raise some questions about priorities. The small group is best seen as an essential component of the church's structure and ministry, not as a replacement for the church.

Jess Moody says, "We will win the world when we realize that fellowship, not evangelism, must be our primary emphasis. When we demonstrate the Big Miracle of Love, it won't be necessary for us to go out—they will come in."[6] I would say rather, our emphasis should be evangelism *through* fellowship, and especially through small *koinonia* groups. This is coupling love's miracle with Christ's invitation.

It is questionable whether the institutional church can have a significant evangelistic ministry today through traditional methods. It may be able to build a denomination and carry out programs, but it will never turn the world rightside up.

Most of today's methods are too big, too slow, too organized, too inflexible, too expensive and too professional ever to be truly dynamic in a fast-paced technological society. If the contemporary church would shake loose from plant and program, from institutionalism and inflexibility, and would return to the dynamic of the early church, it must seriously and self-consciously build its ministry around the small group as basic structure.

The Place of the Small Group in Church Structure Four helpful books which deal with the proper place of small groups in the church are Robert A. Raines' *New Life in the Church,* Lawrence O. Richards' *A New Face for the Church,* and George W. Webber's two books, *God's Colony in Man's World* and *The Congregation in Mission.*[7] (The quotations below from Webber's two books are reprinted by permission of Abingdon Press.)

George Webber was one of the first to see the small group as basic to church structure, as more than just a method. Out of several years' experience in the early days of the East Harlem Protestant Parish, Webber convincingly presents the case for the small group as the basic unit in the life of the congregation. He argues that the small group is not merely another technique; it is something more essential. His analysis is especially relevant because it grows out of experience in an inner-city setting—in a sense, a laboratory for the future.

Webber's insights and experiences are so significant that it is worthwhile to look at them a little more closely. He writes,

A new structure of congregational life is called for which makes provision for genuine meeting between persons, a context in which the masks of self-deception and distrust will be maintained only with difficulty and in which men and women will begin to relate to each other at the level of their true humanity in Christ.[8]

Each local church therefore should "make basic provision for its members to meet in small groups, not as a side light or an option for those who like it, but as a normative part of its life."[9]

Why? In part because of modern patterns of living. In small-town America, and even in urban America in the past, Christians often lived close together in stable communities. But urbanization and technology have changed such patterns, not only in America but in many other parts of the globe. Modern technopolis is a different world. Thanks in part to urban mobility, we live in several distinct worlds in the course of a week: office, shop, neighborhood, school, club. The church is only one world among others for the majority of Christians. Thus today "we do not live in natural, human communities where we know each other in Christ and where, during the week, we have a chance to consider the implications of our faith together. *This must be built into the very structure of the life of the congregation.*"[10]

True, the church often brings believers together at other times than Sunday—but usually only the pious few, and then not in a way that encourages *koinonia.* The average church has no *normative structure* for true sharing and fellowship.

The small group, then, must be both supplemental and normative—supplemental in that it does not replace corporate worship; normative in the sense of being basic church structure, equally important with corporate worship.

Webber expresses this idea in terms of a necessary dual focus for the local congregation. We must maintain the old focus of corporate worship but also insist on the new focus of the small group:

We must participate in the common worship life of the congregation, and we must also participate in a group within that life of the whole congregation in which we seek to understand the meaning of our commitment to Jesus Christ and the implications for our life as colonists in the world.[11]

According to Acts 2:46 the early Christians spent their time "attending the temple together and breaking bread in their homes." "These are the two foci of our life as Christians about which I am speaking," says Webber. "We join in congregational worship. We meet in small groups."[12]

Thus the small group is not an optional method; it is essential structure. Notes Webber,

Experience in many places suggests that such meetings must be both normative for a congregation and regular. The moment they become the possession of a pious few they are likely to lose momentum. This is not to suggest that a majority of the congregation will necessarily participate, but it does mean that the expected pattern for the congregation, shared in by the responsible leadership, does focus on small groups. The important point is that the small unit be seen, not as a temporary expedient or special form, but as an essential structure of congregational life in our day.[13]

Groups Exist for Service But the mere existence of small groups is not enough. Their function must be clearly understood. Their purpose is objective, not merely subjective. If the focus is only on personal spiritual growth the groups turn inward and become self-defeating—like regularly pulling up a plant by the roots to see if it is growing. Rather, the purpose of such groups "must be defined in objective terms that involve work to be done and goals to be achieved."[14] They exist for service; they are "enabling groups" for Christian obedience in the world.

For the purpose of obedience and service, the small groups set before themselves the objective task of Bible study. The crucial fact is that something happens in Bible study in a small group that does not happen elsewhere. The Holy Spirit gives the unique gift of *koinonia* which makes Bible study come alive. Thus Webber has discovered,

People who have listened politely to sermons for years, when they gather together to listen to God's word from the Bible, are most likely to squirm in the face of honest confrontation, and only with difficulty can they brush aside the demands upon their lives.[15]

This awakening may not happen immediately, however.

Webber as well as others have noted that weeks or months may pass before miracles happen. Says Robert Coleman, "The members must be honest with God and with each other. It may take awhile to come to this freedom and trust. After all, you are not prone to bare your soul to people you do not know."[16] Partially for this reason the small group must be essential church structure, not merely a tentative experiment. *Koinonia* is not to be experimented with, but to be experienced.

The Small Group and Church Institutionalism One of the most promising aspects of the small group is just at this point of its possibilities as basic structure. The small group offers some hope of a way through the suffocating institutionalism of the modern church. The average local church is weighed down with excess organizational baggage which at the same time seems unavoidable. What to do? How does one find a pattern for congregational life which is "functional for mission"?

In a passage of potentially great significance for today's search for a more relevant ecclesiology, Webber writes,

The clear demand of mission is that the multiplicity of congregational organizations be eliminated. A missionary congregation does not need a women's missionary society, but women engaged in mission. For male fellowship let the men join the Rotary or the union and in that context become salt that preserves the secular structures of community. . . . The small groups in a congregation, along with the vestry, session, or governing board, can manage to fulfill the necessary institutional requirements of the congregation without setting up a host of organizations to fill out in full a denominational table of organization for the local church. . . .

Thus we conclude that congregational organization must be functional for mission. The time in small groups must have one eye always on the worldly involvements of their members, so that the precious time the church requires will be used for equipping the saints.[17]

For illustration, Webber mentions the annual every-member canvass commonly used to underwrite the church budget. Usually this involves considerable time and organization. But several inner-city churches have conducted the canvass through existing Bible study groups that already reached into most parish homes—a system remarkably similar to that of the early Wesleyan "class meetings" in England. The objective was reached at considerable savings of time and effort. Says Webber, "It sounds simple and is simple."[18]

The small group can become basic structure in a local church if there is the vision for it and the will to innovate. The change cannot come, however, without rethinking traditional programs and structures. The midweek prayer meeting may have to go in favor of a number of midweek small group meetings so that the small groups do not take up another precious weeknight or become something merely tacked on. Other traditional services and activities may be replaced by small group meetings. In fact, the whole organization of the church's life may require review.

The small group is not a panacea. No effort of man can bring the church to greater faithfulness in meeting the needs and problems of its day except as the Holy Spirit directs and infills. But the small group is an essential component of the church's structure and life. In order for men to be moved by the Holy Spirit there must be an openness toward God and toward others, an openness which best develops in a context of the supporting love and fellowship of other sincere seekers after God.

In the early days of the great Wesleyan Revival in England two hundred years ago, John Wesley discovered the importance of the small group for his day. He instituted small cell groups—"class meetings"—for the conservation of converts. He soon saw significant results. In reply to criticism of the method he wrote,

Many now happily experienced that Christian fellowship which they had not so much as an idea before. They began to "bear one another's

burdens," and naturally to "care for each other." As they had daily a more intimate acquaintance with, so they had a more endeared affection for, each other.[19]

In short, the early Methodists discovered the *koinonia* of the Holy Spirit through the use of small groups. The wineskins were useful for the wine. Nothing was more typical of the Methodist Revival than a dozen or so persons meeting together in private homes.

The Bible does not prescribe any particular pattern of church organization. But the practical necessities of our day suggest the need for small groups as basic to church structure.

12

CHURCH AND CULTURE

The Bible paints a distinct profile of what the church is intended to be and gives the early history of the church in two cultural contexts: Palestinian Jewish society and first-century Graeco-Roman society. On the basis of this biblical witness, the church in each epoch faces the task of forming those wineskins most compatible with its nature and mission within its particular culture.

But here we face a prickly problem. We see that biblically the church is the people of God and the fellowship of the Holy Spirit, not an organizational institution. But when we look at the contemporary church, we see not only (or even primarily) the church as people; we find also a proliferation of denominations, institutions, agencies, associations and buildings to which the name *church* is applied. The Bible does not speak of such institutions and structures. They clearly have no explicit biblical basis. How do we handle such structures in the light of the biblical picture of the church?

We face here the problem of *culture.* Both organizational patterns and architecture are expressions of particular cultural values and norms. How can we, in a practical way, maintain a biblical understanding of the church while the church embodies itself in such a vast array of diverse, culturally colored wineskins?

Drawing on the emphases of the previous chapters, I would

like now to outline the biblical view of the church as I understand it, relating this particularly to the problems of *culture* and *structure*. This chapter thus serves as a summary of all that I have attempted to say to this point.

Donald McGavran speaks of "the magnificent and intricate mosaic of mankind" represented by the world's cultures and emphasizes that "adaptation of Christianity to the culture of each piece of the mosaic is crucially important." Thus the goal of the church is "to multiply, in every piece of the magnificent mosaic, truly Christian churches which fit that piece, are closely adapted to *its* culture, and recognized by *its* non-Christians as 'our kind of show.' "[1] This is happening today in a remarkable way. The Body of Christ is amazingly and gloriously diverse, and increasingly so as the gospel fire leaps cultural walls and spreads to peoples who have never heard.

As this happens, however, the question of culture becomes crucial for the church. How does one deal with the problem of wineskins in a situation of increasing cultural diversity?

Traditional Views of the Church It is common to speak of the *visible church* and the *invisible church*. While this distinction is not wholly satisfactory, it does help resolve a problem always before us: the painful contrast between what the church is called to be (the holy, righteous people of God) and what it too often in fact is (an unholy, cantankerous organization of men). By making the visible-invisible distinction, at least we can say that there really is a holy, spiritual, God-directed church that transcends what the eye normally sees.

The biblical view of the church may be contrasted with two traditional views which correspond roughly to the visible church—invisible church distinction.[2] These are the *institutional view* and the *mystical view*.

The institutional view identifies the visible institutional structure with the essence of the church and makes no significant distinction between the two. Thus most denominations are called *churches,* and in practice *church* and *denomination* mean the same thing.

Although this view reached its most elaborate form in Roman Catholicism, it is also common among Protestants. In Protestantism, however, it does not represent so much a theoretical or theological position as it does common, popular usage. On reflection, many would doubtless say the institution is not the same thing as the church, and the idea of the invisible church would be brought in. But in fact popular usage does not make this distinction, and *church* is equated with the organizational structure.

There may be nothing wrong with calling denominations or institutional structures *churches*—but this is not what the Bible means by *church*! When Paul or Peter or Jesus Christ say *church,* they clearly do not refer to an institution or organization. That is not what *visible church* would have meant to the apostles.[3]

In contrast, the mystical view puts the church far above space, time and sin as an ethereal reality comprising all true believers in Christ and known only to God. It is therefore invisible, in the sense that its precise limits are unknown to any man. The mystical view attempts to solve the problem of the embarrassing disparity between the institutional, or visible, church and the church as biblically described. It is a little like Plato's theory of ideas: What we see may be imperfect, but a perfect church exists invisibly.

There is, of course, an invisible church, or rather we should say, the true church of Christ surpasses visible reality. But this also is not what the Bible normally means by *church.* While the Bible does speak of the great multitude of the saved from every nation and every age who comprise the one true church, this is not the common meaning of *church* in the New Testament; nor is the meaning in Scripture a highly mystical concept. There may be an invisible church, but such an immaterial conception is not very helpful in understanding the life and growth of the church on earth and in history. When the Bible says *church,* it does not normally mean an invisible, ethereal reality divorced from space and time any more than it means an institutional organization.

Both these views have one thing in common: They fail to take culture seriously. In the institutional view the church becomes so wedded to its particular culture that the culturally determined nature of much of its life and structure is unperceived. Thus the church becomes culture-bound. This creates problems especially when cultures change or when cross-cultural evangelism is attempted.

In the mystical view, however, the church floats nebulously *above* culture and never becomes involved in the limiting dimensions of space, time and history. Cultural factors, which affect theology, structures and evangelism, are not taken into account.

Thus both the institutional view and the mystical view are inadequate. Both cloud the clear biblical meaning of the church—one by too close an identification of the church with culture, the other by a removal of the church from culture. In both cases it is really culture which becomes "invisible."

To understand the church biblically we must move beyond the traditional visible-invisible conception and move back to the prior and more fundamental biblical view. We must take the church seriously in such a way that space, time and history (the dimensions of culture) are also taken seriously.

How the Bible Sees the Church In contrast to traditional views, the Bible describes the church in the midst of culture, struggling to maintain its fidelity while tainted by the corrosive acids of paganism and Jewish legalism. This view is sharply relevant for the modern age. We will look briefly at three essential aspects of the biblical view.

1. *The Bible sees the church in cosmic-historical perspective.* Scripture places the church at the very center of God's cosmic

purpose. This is seen most clearly in Paul's writings, and particularly in the book of Ephesians. Paul was concerned to speak of the church as the result of, and within the context of, the plan of God for his whole creation (Eph. 1:9-10, 20-23; 3:10; 6:12).[4]

What is this cosmic plan? Based on the first three chapters of Ephesians we may say it is that God may glorify himself by uniting all things in Christ through the church. The key idea is clearly *reconciliation*—not only the reconciliation of man to God, but the reconciliation of all things, "things in heaven and things on earth" (Eph. 1:10). Central to this plan is the reconciliation of man to God through the blood of Jesus Christ. But the reconciliation Christ brings extends to all the alienations that result from man's sin: between man and himself, between man and man, and between man and his physical environment. As mind-boggling as the thought is, Scripture teaches that this reconciliation even includes the redemption of the physical universe from the effects of sin as everything is brought under proper headship in Jesus Christ.[5]

Paul emphasizes the fact of *individual* and *corporate* salvation through Christ, and from this goes on to place personal salvation in cosmic perspective. The redemption of persons is the *center* of God's plan, but it is not the *circumference* of that plan. Paul alternates between a close-up and a long-distance view, for the most part focusing on the close-up of personal redemption, but periodically switching to a long-distance, wide-angle view that takes in "all things"—things visible and invisible; things past, present and future; things in heaven and things on earth; all the principalities and powers—the whole cosmic-historical scene.[6]

Historically, the people of God have disagreed not so much over *what* God is doing in the world but over *when* he will do it. Most Christians admit that, in one sense or another, God is bringing history to a cosmic climax. But one branch has said, "Not now; *then*!" And, in reaction, another group has said,

"Not then; *now*!" Those who postpone any real presence of the kingdom until after Christ's return ("Not now; *then*") do not expect any substantial renewal now except in the realm of individual human experience—not in politics, art, education, culture in general, and not even, really, in the church. On the other side are those who so emphasize present renewal in society in general that both personal conversion and the space-time future return of Christ are denied or overshadowed, and man's deep sinfulness is not taken seriously.

Hopefully, Christians today throughout the world are coming to see that the kingdom of God is neither entirely present nor entirely future. The kingdom of God (the uniting of all things in Jesus Christ) is *now here,* is *coming* and *will come.* Francis Schaeffer well expresses this balanced view when he speaks of a "substantial healing" now in all the areas of sin-caused alienation. Christians are not to put all real reconciliation off into an eschatological future; neither are they to expect total perfection now. What God promises is a substantial healing now and a total healing after Christ's return.[7] Putting this fact in terms of God's cosmic plan, we may say that God has *already* begun the reconciliation of all things in human history.

What, then, is the role of the church in God's cosmic plan? According to Ephesians 3:10, God's will is that "*through the church* the manifold wisdom of God might now be made known to the principalities and powers in the heavenly places." The church is the earthly agent of the cosmic reconciliation God wills. God is bringing about his cosmic purpose through the instrumentality of the church. This means the church's mission is broader than evangelism. Evangelism is at the center of the church's role as agent of reconciliation, and therefore is the first priority. But the mission of the church extends to reconciliation in other areas as well.

German missiologist Peter Beyerhaus clarifies the church's role in God's cosmic purpose when he says the church is "the new messianic community of the kingdom." Says Beyerhaus,

"The messianic kingdom presupposes a messianic community." Thus the church in the world "is the transitory communal form" of the kingdom of God "in the present age, and through his church Christ exercises a most important ministry towards the visible coming of the kingdom." So the church is God's earthly agent of his coming reign. Beyerhaus defines this kingdom as "God's redeeming lordship successively winning such liberating power over the hearts of men, that their lives and thereby finally the whole creation (Rom. 8:21) become transformed into childlike harmony with his divine will."[8]

This is the cosmic perspective in which the Bible sees the church. The kingdom of God is coming, and to the extent this coming takes place in space-time history before the return of Christ, it is to be accomplished through the people of God.

2. *The Bible sees the church in charismatic, rather than institutional, terms.* According to the New Testament, the church is a charismatic organism, not an institutional organization. The church is the result of the grace (Greek, *charis*) of God. It is through grace that the church is saved (Eph. 2:8) and through the exercise of spiritual gifts of grace (*charismata*) that the church is edified (Rom. 12:6-8; Eph. 4:7-16; 1 Pet. 4:10-11). Thus the church is, by definition, *charismatic.* As Clark Pinnock observes, "According to Scripture, the Church *is* a charismatic community."[9]

The church's essential characteristic is life, as suggested by biblical figures for the church. Its life is an organized life, to be sure; but this organization is secondary and derivative. It is the result of life. The church is, first of all, a spiritual organism, which may, secondarily, have some organizational expressions.

The New Testament and the writings of the first church fathers show that the early church saw itself as a charismatic community, not as an organization or institution. "Most church historians agree that the apostolic church was a charismatic, spiritual fellowship," says Donald Bloesch.[10] With the gradual institutionalization of the church, however, the idea of the church as an organization became more prominent and largely crowded out the charismatic-organic view, especially in the West, where Roman views of law and the state had their influence on the church. Thus "in the history of theology the Church as assembled community of the faithful has been too often neglected in favor of the Church as institution," notes Roman Catholic theologian Hans Küng.[11]

In the biblical view, God gives his gracious gift of salvation on the basis of Christ's work and through the agency of the Holy Spirit. This provides the basis of the church's community life. The pure light of God's "manifold grace"[12] is then refracted as it shines through the church, producing the varied, many-colored *charismata.* This provides the basis for the church's diversity within unity. The church is edified through the exercise of spiritual gifts as "the whole body, joined and knit together by every joint with which it is supplied, . . . makes bodily growth and upbuilds itself in love" (Eph. 4:16).

This is important in order to have a healthy, growing church. In order for the church to reach its true, biblical potential, it must be based on a charismatic model, not an institutional model. Churches which structure themselves charismatically are largely prepared for the future. But churches which are encased in rigid, bureaucratic, institutional structures may soon find themselves trapped in culturally bound forms which are fast becoming obsolete.

3. *The Bible sees the church as the community of God's people.* The essential biblical figures of body and bride of Christ, household, temple or vineyard of God, and so forth, give us the basic idea of the church. But these are metaphors and not a definition. I believe the most biblical definition is to say that the church is the community of God's people.[13] The two key elements here are the church as a *people*, a new race or humanity, and as a *community,* or fellowship. We have already dis-

cussed these two sides of the church in chapters 7 and 8.

People and community are two poles which together make up the biblical reality of the church. On the one hand, the church is the people of God. This concept, with rich Old Testament roots, underlines the objective fact of God's acting throughout history to call and prepare "a chosen race, a royal priesthood, a holy nation, God's own people" (1 Pet. 2:9). Here the emphasis is on the *universality* of the church—God's people scattered throughout the world in hundreds of specific denominations, movements and other structures. Seen in cosmic-historical perspective, the church is the people of God.

On the other hand, the church is a community or fellowship, a *koinonia*. This emphasis, found more in the New Testament, grows directly out of the experience of Pentecost. If peoplehood underlines the continuity of God's plan from Old to New Testament, community calls attention to the "new covenant," the "new wine," the "new thing" God did in the resurrection of Jesus Christ and the Spirit's baptism at Pentecost. The emphasis here is on the *locality* of the church in its intense, interactive community life at the level of the local congregation. Seen as a charismatic organism, the church is the community of the Holy Spirit.

The church, then, is the community of God's people. It is a charismatic organism established by God as the agent of his plan for human history. As such, it is cross-culturally valid and can be implanted and grow in any human culture.

Church Structure in Cross-Cultural Perspective If the church is the community of God's people, what shall we say then about the diverse institutions, organizations, denominations and architectural structures which we commonly include under the umbrella *church*? How do such structures relate to the church as God's community?

The two most common tendencies have been either to say that these structures are actually a part of the essence of the church, and thus "sacralize" them,[14] or else to take an anti-institutional stance and insist that all such structures are invalid and must be abandoned. A more helpful option, however, is to view all such structures as para-church structures which exist alongside of and parallel to the community of God's people, but are not themselves the church. These structures are useful to the extent they aid the church in its mission, but are man-made and culturally determined. Whereas the church itself is part of the new wine of the gospel, all para-church structures are wineskins—useful, at times indispensable, but also subject to wear and decay. The church is the community of God's people, and this is what the Bible means by *church.* The church can be nothing other than this! Institutional structures, then, are best seen as something different from the church—potentially useful aids to the church's life and ministry, but never a part of the essence of the church.

Normally, para-church structures have been thought of as extradenominational or interdenominational organizations such as the Billy Graham Evangelistic Association or the National Association of Evangelicals. Denominations themselves are not usually thought of as para-church structures. But since the church biblically understood is always people and can only be people, therefore any institutional structure, whether a denomination, a mission agency, a Christian college, an evangelical publishing house or an evangelistic association, is a para-church structure. In other words, from the biblical standpoint, both an evangelistic association and a denominational organization are para-church structures, while the communities of believers within these structures are the church. Para-church structures, including denominations, may be legitimate and necessary, but are not the church. This conclusion seems to me inescapable in the light of biblical teachings about the church's essential being.

Does this mean that all structures are para-church structures, that no structures are themselves part of the essence of the church? Not necessarily. The church is a body and therefore is structured as a body. Thus to be biblically valid any structures which are truly *church* structures can only be structures which are charismatic and organic. Anything else is a para-church structure. Institutional and organizational structures may have their validity as para-church structures, but should not be confused with the church as the community of God's people. The Bible itself does give us some principles about the organic structure of the church, and some basic church structures are discernible in the life of the New Testament church. I have already mentioned these in previous chapters, and in a moment I will summarize them.

I want to suggest first, however, that several benefits come from distinguishing between the church and para-church structures: (1) That which is always cross-culturally relevant (the biblically understood church) is distinguished from that which is culturally bound and determined (para-church structures). Thus one is free to see the church as *culturally relevant and involved* and yet not as culturally bound. (2) One is free also to modify para-church structures as culture changes, for these are not themselves the church and therefore are largely culturally rather than biblically determined. (3) Finally, this distinction makes it possible to see a *wide range of legitimacy* in denominational confessions and structures. If such structures are not themselves the church and are culturally determined, then whole volumes of controversy and polemics lose their urgency and become merely secondary. Widely varying confessions are freed (at least potentially) to concentrate on that which unites them—being the people of God and carrying out their kingdom tasks—while relegating structural differences to the plane of cultural and historical relativity. Thus the crucial consideration for structure becomes not *biblical legitimacy* but *functional relevancy.*

Figure 1 suggests further implications of this distinction between the church and para-church structures.

The Church	Para-Church Structures
1. God's creation	1. Man's creation
2. Spiritual fact	2. Sociological fact
3. Cross-culturally valid	3. Culturally bound
4. Biblically understood and evaluated	4. Sociologically understood and evaluated
5. Validity determined by spiritual qualities and fidelity to Scripture	5. Validity determined by function in relation to the mission of the church
6. God's agent of evangelism and reconciliation	6. Man's agents for evangelism and service
7. Essential	7. Expendable
8. Eternal	8. Temporal and temporary
9. Given by divine revelation	9. Shaped by human tradition
10. Purpose: to glorify God	10. Purpose: to serve the church

Figure 1. Differences between the Church and Para-church Structures

Guidelines for Church Structure From the biblical picture of the church we can now distill three fundamental principles for structure. I believe these principles provide a basic biblical foundation for church structure in any cultural context and help lead to effective witness and growth.[15]

1. *Leadership should be based on the exercise of spiritual gifts.* Hierarchical or organizational patterns must not be permitted to obscure or overwhelm the basic biblical pattern of charismatic (that is, Spirit-appointed and endowed) leadership.

In the New Testament, leadership was at first provided by the original eleven apostles, and later by Paul and an expanding group of other apostles, prophets, evangelists, pastors, teachers, bishops, deacons and elders. All these leadership functions relate to spiritual gifts.[16] It is clear therefore that in the New Testament leadership was based on the exercise of spiritual leadership gifts which were recognized (either formally or informally) by the church.[17]

All spiritual gifts should be emphasized, not just the leadership gifts. But these latter gifts are especially crucial, for their function biblically is precisely to awaken and prepare the other gifts (Eph. 4:11). Thus not only leadership, but the entire life of the church is based on spiritual gifts, or, more precisely, it is based on Christ who awakens spiritual gifts in each member of the community.

2. *The life and ministry of the church should be built on viable large-group and small-group structures.* The early church's common life of worship, fellowship, nurture and witness reveals a dual emphasis—"in the temple and at home"(Acts 5:42). While the community life of the church centered primarily in the home, worship and nurture took place both in the temple and in small, house gatherings (Acts 2:42, 46-47; 4:34-35; 5:25, 42).[18] Although worship in the Jewish temple eventually ceased, both large- and small-group gatherings seem to have marked the common life of the early church throughout the Mediterranean world.[19]

These were the two foci of early church life: the large congregation and the small group. This was also the pattern the disciples had followed with Jesus. For two or three years the disciples spent much of their time either among outdoor crowds, in the temple or in private small-group conferences with the Master. There was always this small-group—large-group rhythm, the small group providing the intense community life which gave depth to the large-group gatherings.

Theologically, large- and small-group gatherings are the structural implications of the church's being the people of God and the fellowship of the Holy Spirit, as we have already seen. Peoplehood implies the necessity of large-group gatherings while community requires small-group structures.

Church history reveals a recurrent tendency to absolutize

and institutionalize the large group, wedding it to a specific building and form, while at the same time neglecting or even condemning the small group. Virtually every major movement of spiritual renewal in the Christian church has been accompanied by a return to the small group and the proliferation of such groups in private homes for Bible study, prayer and discussion of the faith. Therefore, whatever other structures may be found useful, large-group and small-group structures should be fundamental. Although the specific form of such structures may vary according to culture and circumstances, both are necessary to sustain community and witness. No other structure or form should be allowed to subvert or replace either the large corporate group or the small fellowship group.

The large group and the small group are necessary not only for community and witness but also for discipline. Dean M. Kelley has emphasized in *Why Conservative Churches Are Growing* that discipline, or "strictness," is a characteristic of virtually all significant and society-transforming religious movements. Says Kelley, "A group with evidence of social strength will proportionately show traits of strictness; a group with traits of leniency will proportionately show evidences of social weakness rather than strength."[20]

The gospel makes high demands of all believers and requires ardent discipline. But how is this discipline to be maintained? If the church is truly biblical, such discipline will not be imposed hierarchically but will be internal or intrinsic, enforced by the community itself on the basis of a fund of commonly shared values and under the leadership of the Holy Spirit. The small group is the natural structure for this function. It provides the essential context for perpetuating necessary discipline, for it is the place where common values are found, shared and reinforced. Not only is this sociologically valid, it squares with what Jesus and Paul teach (Mt. 18:15-20; 1 Cor. 5:3-13).

3. *A clear distinction should be made between the church and para-church structures.* Christians must see themselves as the community of God's people, not in the first place as members of an organization. In many a contemporary church this would be revolutionary.

Each church should be helped to understand that institutional structures are legitimate (provided they really aid the church in its life and witness) but not sacred. The important thing, therefore, is not to prescribe which para-church structures should or should not exist in the church, but to insist on the relativity and limitations of such structures.

In summary, the church as the community of God's people should be structured on spiritual gifts of leadership and on some form of large-group and small-group gatherings. Beyond this, the church should take care to distinguish between its essential self and all para-church structures so that it does not become culture-bound, and so that, conversely, in periods of upheaval the wine is not thrown out with the wineskins. This is what happened, essentially, in Russia in 1917, and it could happen on a much wider scale in the future.

These three principles are illustrated in Figure 2.

Implications for Cross-Cultural Witness Several conclusions for the church's worldwide, cross-cultural witness follow from the foregoing discussion:

1. *The church as biblically presented is always cross-culturally relevant.* This is true because the church is a cosmic-historical, charismatic organism that proceeds from divine action and transcends any particular cultural form. Since created by God, at its deepest level it corresponds to the structure of what is, the structure of reality as God made it.

2. *Similarly, the basic structures of charismatic leadership and small-group–large-group gatherings are always cross-culturally viable.* This follows from the foregoing analysis and has also been abundantly demonstrated throughout church history

and in the modern missionary age.

3. *On the other hand, para-church structures are not necessarily cross-culturally valid.* Since these are culturally determined, particular para-church structures will be transferable from one culture to another only to the extent that the two cultures are compatible. Basic adaptations will often have to be made.

4. *The exercise of spiritual gifts will result in cross-cultural evangelism.* Since the beginning of the church and through the

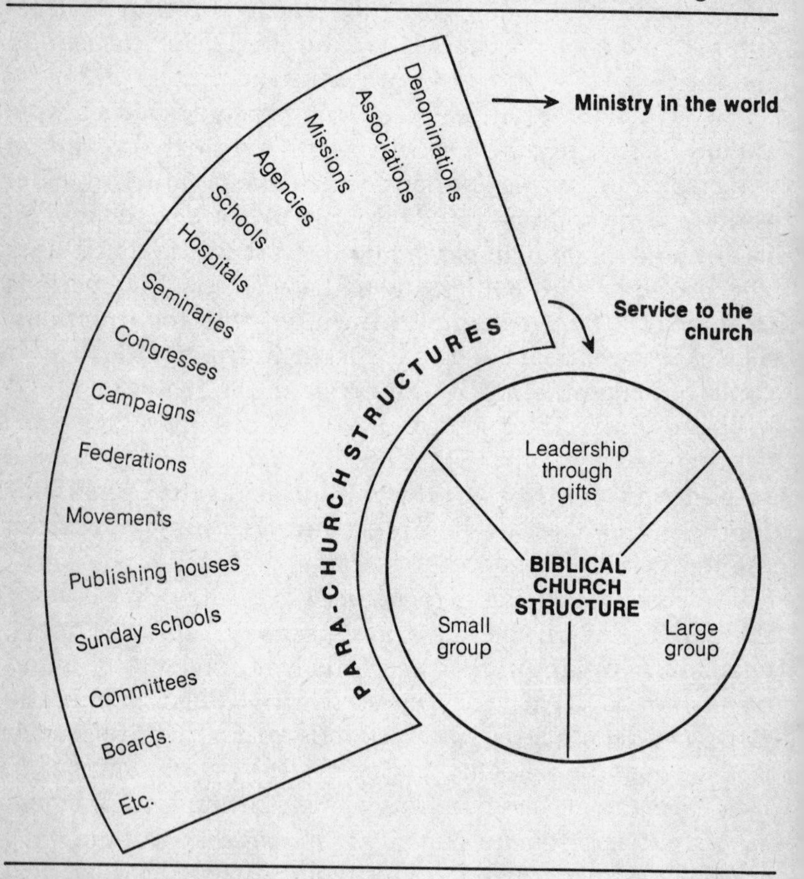

Figure 2. A Model for Church Structure

ages, God has been calling and sending out his charismatically equipped missionaries. Paul related his own missionary ministry to the charismatic gift he had received (Eph. 3:7-8). The Antiochian pattern (Acts 13:1-4) has been repeated countless times and will continue to be repeated until Christ returns (Mt. 24:14). It is God who calls and who gives gifts, and the gift and the call go together.

5. *The church is itself a missionary structure, and any group of missionaries may be a legitimate embodiment of the church.* This means there can be no question of the church versus "missionary structures." Where missionaries are, there is the church; and there missionaries are responsible to demonstrate the reality of Christian community. The real point of tension therefore is between the church as the community of God's people and institutional expressions of the church. If Christ is really in them, missionaries can never go to another culture and leave the church behind. But they can, and often should, leave behind or modify the para-church forms peculiar to their own culture.

6. *On the other hand, para-church missionary/evangelistic structures should be created wherever necessary to get the job done.* While the church is God's agent for cosmic reconciliation, dynamic para-church structures can be man's agents of reconciliation, useful in God's hands for the more rapid and effective spread of the kingdom. Denominational groups should freely collaborate with other para-church organizations which are doing work they themselves cannot do or which will help them carry on their own witness. Such organizations, however, should always be directed ultimately toward the formation and edification of the church (though in widely different ways) or the extension of the church's ministry, while not allowing themselves to be confused with the church or become ends in themselves.

7. *Since they are man-made and culturally determined, all para-church structures should be subjected to continuous, rigorous socio-*

logical and theological analysis to determine their fidelity to the biblical concept of the church and their effectiveness as instruments of the church. We should not hesitate to make the most exacting sociological studies of mission agencies, evangelistic movements, denominational structures and so forth. Some para-church structures should be devoted exclusively to this task (which is, in a sense, what World Vision's Missions Advanced Research and Communications Center is doing). History teaches us that many ecclesiastical structures will eventually succumb to institutionalism and become hindrances rather than helps to the church. The fact that God has raised up a movement is no warranty against eventual infidelity or self-centeredness. Having clearly distinguished such structures from the essence of the church, we can freely ask to what extent these forms are actually functional.

The better sort of such para-church organizations will welcome this kind of evaluation and may even provide for it themselves. Those para-church groups which are nervous about such study are often the very ones most needing it.

There is no salvation outside the church unless the Body of Christ be decapitated, separated from the Head; for when one is regenerated he becomes a part of the Body of Christ. The church *is* the Body of Christ, the community of the Holy Spirit, the people of God. As such, it is the agent of God's plan for the reconciliation of all things in Jesus Christ. The need of the hour is to understand the church as a Spirit-endowed charismatic organism which is cross-culturally valid, not as an institutional organization molded by the world. Once this distinction is made, the normal growth and witness of the church can be understood and planned for, and the various para-church structures, including denominations, can be dealt with and used effectively.

13
A LESSON FROM HISTORY

Does history provide any precedents for the vision of the church and church structure presented in the foregoing chapters? Where in space and time do we find a happy and vital union of gospel wine and church wineskins? Where has a clear gospel vision been coupled with viable structures to produce not only personal conversion but true community and cultural renewal as well?

We have already made reference to the radical wing of the Reformation and the movements that arose from it (chap. 3). These movements had their undeniable impact, but were unsuccessful in bringing about a thoroughgoing reform of both the church and society.

Carl F. H. Henry, in making "a plea for evangelical demonstration," cites two more recent historical precedents: the Wesleyan Revival in eighteenth-century England and the evangelical awakening in the Netherlands at the turn of this century under the leadership of Abraham Kuyper.[1] There are several good reasons for restudying both Wesley and Kuyper. Although standing in different Protestant traditions, both Kuyper and Wesley were used by God for righteousness to such a marked degree that contemporary Christians ought to be asking *why*.

My own tradition places me closer to John Wesley, and I have been struck in recent years by the church's growing rediscovery of his relevance for today. One can hardly pick up a book by an evangelical author without finding some reference to him. When contemporary writers wish to point out that evangelicals have historically had a social conscience, Wesley is cited. When the need for simple gospel preaching is emphasized, Wesley is given as an example. The fact is that Wesley illustrates several qualities that are essential for Christian faithfulness in techno-urban society. I would like to deal with these in this chapter.

The Wesleyan Revival witnessed perhaps the most thoroughgoing transformation of a society by the gospel in history—a fact particularly important for the modern church since the Wesleyan Revival occurred during the period of upheaval which accompanied the Industrial Revolution in England.

It is probably true that the socio-political effects of the Wesleyan Revival have often been overdrawn. The thesis that Wesley saved England from a French-style political revolution is, at best, highly speculative and ignores important differences between the French and English cultures of the eighteenth century.[2] Yet it is true that social conditions in England improved dramatically during the course of the century, and the Wesleyan Revival was a major factor in this change.

Wherein lies the relevance of John Wesley for the contemporary church? What were the factors that accounted for his impact?

Of the many factors which could be cited, six are especially relevant for today. Three of these relate to Wesley's message and three to his method.

John Wesley's Message John Wesley had a message, and he was not ashamed of it. Wesley had something definite and specific to communicate, and the message was communicable in human language—a fact which needs emphasizing in our age. What were the principal elements of this message?

1. *A clear proclamation of the fact of personal salvation through Jesus Christ.* Wesley's message was salvation by faith. He emphasized the basic biblical teachings of man's sin and lostness, Christ's sacrifice and resurrection, and the transformation of the new birth.

There were those in Wesley's day who said such a message was no longer relevant. People would not listen. But the public response to his preaching undermined the critics. People listened and responded by the thousands.

We must emphasize that Wesley's was a *clear* proclamation of the basic gospel. Though an Oxford scholar, he had no patience with high-sounding phrases that failed to communicate. It is said that Wesley would often preach newly prepared sermons to his maid, a simple, uneducated girl, and have her stop him whenever she did not understand his words. His passion was to communicate with the masses.

This was the same Wesley who, preaching at Oxford, might quote from Latin authors or from the Greek New Testament. Wesley was a scholar, but he put his scholarship at the service of the people.

2. *A consistent emphasis on the Spirit-filled life.* Wesley constantly emphasized the need for the filling and continuing ministry of the Holy Spirit in the life of the believer, and thousands of early Methodists found the experience a reality. In nearly every city he visited, Wesley carefully examined the members of the Methodist societies about their Christian experience. Although he frequently found spiritual counterfeits, he also found much spiritual reality and power. The Holy Spirit was at work.

Wesley emphasized much more than merely a crisis experience of the infilling of the Spirit. His preoccupation was that of Paul: Christian maturity, the edification of the church, the forming of the stature of Christ in each believer. With Wesley there was a constant concern for Christian nurture and growth through the work of the Spirit.

3. *An active and involved social consciousness.* Wesley was supremely an evangelist. And yet, read through a list of his sermon titles or of the pamphlets he published. His topics include wealth, national sins, war, education, medical ethics, the Stamp Act, trade with North America, responsibility to the king, the liquor industry.

There was no question where Wesley stood on poverty and riches, sea piracy, smuggling, the slave trade and other crucial issues of his day. Nor did he think he was compromising his call as an evangelist when he preached on these issues on Sunday morning. He saw, as had the Old Testament prophets, that biblical faith touches every area of life and makes everyone morally responsible, from king to collier.

And the amazing thing is that Wesley's social concern brought results. Why? First, because he awakened a new moral consciousness in the nation. Second, because others followed his example. Third, because as an effective evangelist he was instrumental in transforming thousands of lives. He instilled in his converts the same social concern, thus broadening the popular base for social reform. He proved what the history of the church in other times and places shows: There is no combination more potent in transforming society than biblical evangelism coupled with biblical social concern—the joining of Old Testament prophet and New Testament evangelist.

Wesley himself did more than just talk about social reform. Among other things, he agitated for prison, liquor and labor reform; set up loan funds for the poor; campaigned against the slave trade and smuggling; opened a dispensary and gave medicines to the poor; worked to solve unemployment; and personally gave away considerable sums of money to persons in need.[3]

John Wesley's Method But John Wesley's message is only part of the story. He saw—or rather, learned—that the clearest, most biblical proclamation of the gospel often has little effect if it is locked within the walls (literal or figurative) of the institutional church. And it is here that Wesley becomes especially relevant for the problem of wineskins.

Others before and since have preached as clearly and effectively as Wesley, but with not half the abiding results. Why? In part, because their message was encrusted in rigid unbiblical ideas about the nature of the church.

Wesley started out strictly "high church" in his ecclesiology, but God did not let him stay there. To a considerable degree he was still a high churchman at his death, but in many ways he learned to be remarkably flexible and unconventional. This can be illustrated by three aspects of Wesley's ministry:

1. *He did not restrict himself to the institutional church.* John Wesley's effectiveness dates from the time he began carrying the gospel outside the four walls of the church.

It happened like this: Wesley's friend, the evangelist George Whitefield, had a large congregation of coal miners at Kingswood, near Bristol, where Whitefield was preaching regularly. Whitefield's ministry was "field preaching"—assembling a large crowd in an open field and there opening the Word. Wesley frowned on this at first, for he had been, in his words, "so tenacious of every point relating to decency and order that I should have thought the saving of souls a sin if it had not been done in the church."[4]

Whitefield requested—practically insisted—that Wesley take over his congregation so he could return to America. Wesley did not want to accept, but after seeing Whitefield's ministry, he felt the call was from God: "At four in the afternoon, I submitted to be more vile, and proclaimed in the highways the glad tidings of salvation, speaking from an eminence in a ground adjoining to the city, to about three thousand people."[5]

The crowds grew, and soon there were congregations in other places—in fact, within a few years, throughout England,

Scotland and Ireland. Wesley had discovered that when the people stop coming to the church, it is time for the church to go to the people.

Wesley, his brother Charles and Whitefield did not win popular praise for their efforts. Bishop Leslie R. Marston notes, "These three men were called mad enthusiasts because they would free the gospel from the confining gothic arches of established religion and release it to the masses in street and field, to the sick and unclean in hovel and gutter, to the wretched and condemned in Bedlam and prison."[6]

Wesley was a devout churchman. He had no intention of founding a new dissenting group; he urged his hearers and new converts to attend the regular Anglican services. He never preached in field or marketplace at the same hour as stated worship services.

But Wesley was also a realist. He saw that many people simply would not attend the traditional church services, and even those who did failed to receive there all the spiritual help they needed. And this leads us to the second aspect of Wesley's method.

2. *He created new and workable structures for koinonia.* One of the first things Wesley did with his converts was to divide them into groups of a dozen, each group with its own leader. These were the famous Wesleyan "class meetings." Wesley soon discovered the spiritual dynamic of this small group structure.

He said in 1742,

I appointed several earnest and sensible men to meet me, to whom I showed the great difficulty I had long found of knowing the people who desired to be under my care. After much discourse, they all agreed there could be no better way to come to a sure, thorough knowledge of each person than to divide them into classes, like those at Bristol, under the inspection of those in whom I could most confide. This was the origin of our classes in London, for which I can never sufficiently praise God, the unspeakable usefulness of the institution having ever since been more and more manifest.[7]

We have already seen how Wesley later commented that through such small-group participation his followers "began to 'bear one another's burdens' and naturally to 'care for each other,'" coming to an experiential knowledge of genuine Christian fellowship.

Wesley innovated in other aspects of church structure as well—lay ministers (thus providing for the exercise of spiritual gifts), unpretentious "preaching houses" and so forth. He felt free to make such innovations because he conceived of Methodism not as a new denomination but merely as a "society" within the Anglican Church. But regardless of the reasons, he was one of the great innovators in church structure.

Wesley's efforts along this line say much to the contemporary church. Trapped in rigid institutional patterns, today's traditional churches too seldom experience that fellowship of the Holy Spirit of which the New Testament speaks. This was also true of eighteenth-century Anglicanism—and Wesley did something about it.

3. *He preached the gospel to the poor.* One of the most crucial signs of the kingdom is *to whom* the gospel is being ministered. John Wesley, like Jesus, preached to the poor. He sought out those whom no one else was seeking.

Reading his *Journal,* one is impressed with how many times Wesley preached at five a.m. or at midmorning in the marketplace. Why did he often preach at five o'clock? Not for *his* convenience, but for the convenience of the laboring men and women who went to work in mine or factory at daybreak. Wesley assembled the coal miners in the fields before they started work or the crowds in the marketplace at midday. His passion was to preach the gospel to the poor, and among them he had his greatest response.

In short, John Wesley had a message, and he did not muffle it behind stained glass. He went outside the structured church, preaching the gospel to the poor. He refused to allow newborn babes to die of spiritual malnutrition, but provided spiritual homes and foster parents for them. He created new forms of the church—new wineskins—for those who responded. He matched a biblical message with methods in harmony with a biblical ecclesiology.

John Wesley's Secret Was there one special secret behind Wesley's impact? How did Wesley "happen" to find this happy marriage of message and method?

We face here, of course, the mystery of the sovereignty of the Holy Spirit. But we can see at least some of the ways the Spirit worked in Wesley's life.

Wesley was not primarily a theologian, although he was theologically competent. He "theologized" sufficiently to find biblical answers to the basic questions of Christian experience and to confront social issues with biblical revelation. But he never worked out a consistent theological system. His theology was a mixture of high-church traditionalism, believer's church pietism and evangelistic pragmatism. On some questions, such as infant baptism, he never worked out a consistent position but held seemingly contradictory opinions.

There is not even unanimous agreement about whether Wesley was, at heart, an Arminian or a Calvinist! While he has generally been considered an Arminian because of his emphasis on a universal atonement, he was careful not to fall into antinomianism. And there are those who have argued that his theology was basically a variant of Calvinism.[8] If he cannot be neatly classified, it is because he sought to be thoroughly biblical.

So John Wesley's secret did not lie primarily in his theological attainments. It was not essentially theological in this sense. *But it was essentially biblical.* Wesley, the scholar, the author and editor of many books, was "a man of one book"—the Bible. He accepted it implicitly and practiced it consciously. This was his secret: the Word of God.

Wesley held the common-sense view that if the Bible is true, it will show itself true in valid human experience. So his points of reference were, first the Bible, and, secondarily, experience and reason. These were his measures, not church tradition, contemporary philosophy or the opinions of others. What the Bible said was true, regardless of what others thought, and would prove true in human living.

Because he was biblical, Wesley was free to be radical—radical in the proper sense of going back to the roots.

Not that Wesley was without his faults. He was something of an anti-Catholic bigot, although his personal relations with individual Catholics were above reproach. Some will choke on the fact that Wesley was a pro-monarchy political conservative with little patience for upstart American revolutionary radicals, although he sympathized with the colonists at first. But in spite of whatever criticisms are leveled against him, Wesley was at heart a Christian, as all who knew him well testified, and his faith was firmly, radically biblical.

Certainly Wesley had other things going for him besides what I have so far mentioned. He was a gifted administrator and chooser of men (even though some of his chosen leaders later betrayed him). His editing, condensing and publishing of books—a complete library from history to medicine—was a ministry in itself. And he received immeasurable help from his brother Charles, who wrote hundreds of singable hymns which were sung to the popular music of the day.[9] The early Methodists held an intelligible faith partly because they memorized so much of it in the hymns of Charles Wesley!

Each age is unique—but not totally. We can learn much from the past, and especially is this true with regard to the life and structure of the church. There are few periods in the church's past as relevant for today as Wesley's England. And there, too, we find a model of some significance for testing the view of the church and church structure presented in these pages.

14

A LOOK TO THE FUTURE

Someone has said the problem of the present is that the future is not what it used to be. It's true! We are now living under the "pressure of the future" in a way that has never before been true during the history of man's pilgrimage on planet Earth.

Man today is moving into a kind of society that is qualitatively different from anything yet experienced by human personality. Although this time of ferment and transition shows marked similarities to the first-century Roman world, it is bringing man to a situation unprecedented in history. Man himself has not changed drastically, but human culture has evolved to the point where man finds himself in a substantially different world. Needless to say, this fact has tremendous implications for the church and its structure.

Many are inclined to doubt that the world is fundamentally different today. Unconsciously reaching for stability, we prefer to think that society is not basically dissimilar from what it was in the past: It is merely more intense, moving more quickly! But empirical evidence reveals a more unsettling picture.

Alvin Toffler assembles an impressive array of fact and opinion in support of the uniqueness of the modern age in his book *Future Shock.* Toffler points out that "a growing body of reputable opinion asserts that the present movement represents nothing less than the second great divide in human history, comparable in magnitude only with that first great break in historic continuity, the shift from barbarism to civilization."[1] And Toffler cites economist Kenneth Boulding's comment that "as far as many statistical series related to mankind are concerned, the date that divides human history into two equal parts is well within living memory. . . . I was born in the middle of human history, to date, roughly. Almost as much has happened since I was born as happened before."[2]

The key facts here are the cumulative impact of technology and the resulting acceleration of change. What has happened within the lifetime of every person who will read this book is that the rate of change has so rocketed upward that more change—and more *significant* change—takes place within one year than occurred in literally hundreds of previous years. And the rate continues to rise. This means that, unless there is a major catastrophe to stop this spiral, the few years between now and the year 2000 will see more change than has occurred since Abraham left Ur of the Chaldees. It will be as though all the political, scientific, industrial, social and religious revolutions of the past four thousand years were crowded into one short lifetime.

An Accelerating World Perhaps the two most eloquent symbols of the new age are the billboard and the TV commercial. Both tell us much about the kind of world we and our children will inhabit.

Both the billboard and the commercial are increasingly ubiquitous. Wherever one goes one is bombarded by their messages, and the images they project are nearly inescapable. This is symptomatic of the monolithic, pervasive, dynamic culture being formed today. It is inescapable, as I saw every time I drove along one of São Paulo's busy expressways; it is insistent. There is no "refuge from the world"; there is no private world any longer. It is not necessary for Big Brother to see us. It is sufficiently harassing for us always to see Big Brother and receive his messages! And today Big Brother is not the government or some political leader; he is computerized, nearly autonomous technology.

A second trait of the billboard and the commercial is their high degree of transience. Twenty years ago a jingle or advertising slogan might last for years. But the rate of change has so accelerated that now the advertising message, and even the product, lasts only a matter of months or even weeks. The impressive fact is accelerating transience. The billboard is not a permanent structure; it appears or disappears overnight. The message is printed on disposable paper, for it is a disposable message. Today's "urgent" message is discarded tomorrow, replaced by another. This transience is starkly typical of the new age, as Toffler shows. We are increasingly predisposed to think in terms of temporariness, not permanence. Within a year or two much in our lives changes—not merely familiar products, but our car, clothes, reading material and (for an increasing percentage of people) even our homes, friends, jobs, associations and ideas. Contrast this with the lives of most of our grandparents.

Another characteristic of billboards and commercials is their high degree of sophistication. Huge amounts of money and talent go into advertising messages whose life is measured in only weeks of days. It is a joke that TV commercials are often more entertaining than the programs they sponsor, but this is a serious fact and only to be expected when one considers the money and sophisticated planning and analysis that go into every second of TV advertising or every square inch of visual advertising. Ben H. Bagdikian observes, "The most highly paid writers, actors, musicians, and producers in the world are not those that create education for the young, or drama for adults, or political programs for others. They are the men and women who create television commercials."[3]

Advertising is no laughing matter! It is, if anything, one of the most significant facts of the new technoculture, and increasingly so. It shows the shape of the future: society's greatest resources of money and talent being used to transmit a high-impact, high-transience message in order to achieve a specific, predetermined result.

Which leads to another trait of the billboard and TV commercial: their high degree of manipulation. Not only is the advertising message predetermined; it is largely fictitious. The product hailed as "the favorite worldwide" is probably not really such by any empirical criteria. Products do not in fact deliver what the advertisements promise. It would be pitifully naive, however, to suppose they are therefore ineffective. Quite the contrary! They achieve precisely what they are intended to achieve. They "create reality"—that is, an image—that predisposes a significant minority of recipients to respond as intended, normally to buy a particular product or use a particular service.

Political advertising at election time suggests one possible future significance of this tendency toward manipulation and falsification. We are moving into a technological society where planning and predetermination characterize nearly all areas of life.

All of this means that people today are subjected to a higher number of messages, and that these have both greater impact and less truth content. And these tendencies are rapidly accelerating.

These facts are significant in themselves. But I would call attention particularly to the direction they point and to the statement they make about the future.

When we look at the various crises of today—ecological, political, ideological and economic—and then combine these with the fact of acceleration, only one conclusion seems possible: Time is running out. We must face very seriously today the fact that the children being born at the present time will probably be the last generation of humans to inhabit the planet. They may well make up the final generation to reach maturity on Earth.

Such a conclusion is, of course, highly conjectural. Yet there is an impressive array of empirical fact which, if not mixed with a rosy belief in human perfectibility, points ominously in this direction. Let us take a brief look at some of the evidence.

I have already mentioned the increasing transience and rate of change in modern society. The question is, Can the pace accelerate indefinitely? Historian Arnold Toynbee says in his book *Change and Habit,*

In the technological [*realm*], *both progress and the acceleration of progress leap to the eye. At the present time, both are in full swing. Their impetus is unprecedented and portentious. Here, manifestly, we are in the presence of a factor that is confronting Man with a new challenge–the greatest, perhaps, of any that have yet confronted him. Though technology is man-made, it is now challenging Man's ability to retain the power of planning, directing, and controlling his own future by the continuing exercise of the freedom of choice that is one of the distinctive characteristics of human nature. This inanimate apparatus that Man has invented to serve human purposes is now threatening to make a declaration of its independence of its inventor. It is threatening to carry Man whither he would not.*[4]

This fact of acceleration hits us wherever we turn. We are accustomed to seeing population growth graphs shooting vertically off the page. But similar graphs could be drawn in many other areas—the information explosion, energy demand, urbanization, the increase in basic scientific discoveries. Rapid acceleration in increasingly compressed time spans pushes the graphs steadily upward to the point where they approach the vertical. But when the graph line reaches the vertical, *it must end.* Acceleration is not an infinite process; it is finite and eventually must stop or else bring catastrophe. This is seen most clearly in population growth: Either it must slow down *radically,* or it will reach the catastrophe point where space, water, oxygen and food run out. And ultimately it makes little difference which runs out first.

History simply cannot continue to accelerate at an ever-increasing rate. Eventually, something drastic must happen. Our civilization is like a jet airplane, accelerating ever faster and faster. But there is a finite limit to how much speed that airplane can withstand. Unless it slows, it will eventually reach the disintegration point. It is not made to transcend the boundaries of space and time, and neither is man-made culture.

Satan's Final Strategy Given this configuration of developments, the church today should be paying close attention to the Word of God.

Paul warns the church that "we are not contending against flesh and blood, but against the principalities, against the powers, against the world rulers of this present darkness, against the spiritual hosts of wickedness in the heavenly places" (Eph. 6:12).

The battle to end all battles—literally—is on the horizon. And the enemy is not really communism or socialism or materialism; neither is it capitalism or imperialism or the Establishment. It is more subtle still.

The arch enemy is Satan, of course; but like vintage radio's Mr. Chameleon, Satan has a thousand faces. And the church today must be able to unmask him in his two most deceiving contemporary disguises.

The first disguise of the enemy is (for lack of a better term) *spiritism.* Involved here are astrology, the occult, non-Christian mysticism, and such antirational, subjectivist phenomena as drug-taking, Transcendental Meditation and similar behavior. The common denominator here is a turning away from the real world, a turning inward to focus on one's own feelings, mind or inward state. The switch to the outside world is turned off; the inner world is switched on and becomes the only world that matters. As Timothy Leary has said, "Render unto Caesar everything material."

But is this demonic? Yes! Because it splits God's world into two irreconcilable parts and cuts the nerve between thought and action, between the subjective *I* and the objective world. It is deception because it fools a person into thinking that the only world that matters is what goes on inside his own head or body or feelings. It cancels out the possibility of genuine Christian experience, which is both inward and outward. Worse yet, it plays into the hands of Satan's strategy for the last battle.

The other satanic disguise—only gradually and grudgingly coming to be recognized—is *technique*. This is the opposite of spiritism. Its only focus of attention is the outside world, the observable reality. Its only ultimate concern is to find the best possible way to do a thing. But this becomes tyranny, for once the best way is found to build a car, elect a President, sell a product or obtain any other result, all other means are superfluous and doomed to extinction.

Today technique is building a society in which everything depends on technology. A complex technological pryamiding takes place in which ever more advanced technology is necessary to deal with society's problems. The realities of modern technology make ideology obsolete and focus attention on means, not ends. The important question is not Why? but How? And what is technologically possible is therefore good. Technology replaces ideology, and esthetics becomes cosmetics.

But is this satanic? Yes! Because it cancels out all questions of ultimate purpose and meaning, and puts all life on the level of the "penultimate," the next-to-last. In the comfortable world of technique the fundamental questions of why and whither are forgotten. The future may promise a totalitarian technotopia not greatly different from Orwell's *1984* or Huxley's *Brave New World*. Such a possibility is anti-God because it becomes a God-substitute and reduces human significance to the level of the machine.

The church's enemies today are spiritism and technique. Both enslave man, one by locking him inside his own experience (admittedly a wide world but only seemingly transcendent), the other by locking him into a comfortable, colorful, kaleidoscopic room with shrinking walls. In either case, there is finally no escape. Life is either experience without action or action without meaning.

But here comes Satan's dirty trick, and the meaning of the final battle: the marriage of Spiritism and Technique. It looks impossible, but it is happening. Technique is a "clockwork orange," a mechanical sponge. It absorbs everything and reduces culture to methodology, including spiritism and religion.

It is here that *1984* and *Brave New World* were prophetic. In both books a state-controlled, synthetic religion or religion-substitute was provided to put meaning in life and keep all behavior within predictable and thus manageable limits. This insight is much more significant than the question of whether Orwell or Huxley were right or wrong in the details of their respective anti-utopias.

It is here also that today's counter culture has most profoundly deluded itself. The serious drug-users, the communal drop-outs, the Consciousness III children thought they were bringing a new revolution. They were deceived by the kiss of publicity into thinking they were succeeding. But the attention of the media was the kiss of death, and only the first step toward their absorption into the technological society. And behind the curtain one hears the muffled sound of demonic laughter.

For in reality the antirational, the subjective, the experiential pose no threat to technique. The technological society is perfectly willing to make room for the transcendental meditators and the acid heads, as Jacques Ellul has convincingly pointed out.[5] For their introverted world is divorced from action and therefore not really revolutionary. It takes more than "consciousness" to bring off a revolution once technique has the upper hand. Such behavior is even welcome in technotopia, for it keeps the natives quiet, believing they are accomplishing something.

This is Satan's trick, and it suggests the shape of the church's last battle. What happened then to the old enemies of lust, greed, immorality, idolatry, sloth and so forth? They're still around. They're still demonic, and still fully employed. But the principalities and powers under Satan's dominion today are seen particularly in spiritism and technique, gradually merging into one demonic, monolithic plan.

The Church Today and Tomorrow What do these developments mean for the church—for both the wineskins and the wine?

1. *In our present world the whole question of church structure takes on an increasing urgency.* As acceleration increases, only those churches which are structured flexibly and biblically will be able to keep up. These churches will offer the best conditions for the church truly to be the messianic community in these days—and to withstand persecution when it comes.

The church will increasingly have to choose between a charismatic and an institutional, or bureaucratic, model for its life and structure. Technological development, the population explosion and other factors are speeding up the pace of change and squeezing humanity into a potential global ghetto. This acceleration of change puts new strains on all institutional structures.

Alvin Toffler in *Future Shock* argues that "the acceleration of change has reached so rapid a pace that even bureaucracy can no longer keep up." This means that "newer, . . . more instantly responsive forms of organization must characterize the future." We are seeing the "collapse of hierarchy" as "shortcuts that by-pass the hierarchy are increasingly employed" in all kinds of organizations. "The cumulative result of such small changes is a massive shift from vertical to lateral communication systems."[6]

Whether this is good or bad for the church depends on whether the church is structured according to a charismatic or an institutional model. Biblically, it is clear that the church *should* be structured charismatically, and any church so structured already is largely prepared to withstand future shock. But churches which are encased in rigid, bureaucratic, institutional structures may soon find themselves trapped in culturally bound organizational forms which are fast becoming obsolete.[7]

A biblical conception of the church will make clear that the church is essential to the gospel, for it is the Body of Christ. At the same time, it will be clear that man-made institutions and structures are not themselves the church; they are not hallowed. But a biblical *concept* of the church is not enough. Local churches must *incarnate* the biblical reality by structures for worship, witness and common life such as we have been discussing in this book.

2. *The church needs to be watchful* (Mt. 24:42; 1 Thess. 5:6).

These are days when Christians must be clear about what the church *is* and what it *is not*. Just as many false Christs will come in the last days, so many counterfeit and apostate "churches" will litter the spiritual landscape. We must not be led astray by our own fuzzy ideas of the church.

The church must be prepared, both as individuals and as the Christian community, for the lash of persecution and the lure of the antichrist. This means the necessity for both doctrinal clarity and authentic community—for both orthodoxy of belief and orthodoxy of community, to use Francis Schaeffer's phrase.[8] Under the threat of persecution, life in community becomes both more difficult and more essential. Thus the priority of structures which are flexible, mobile, inconspicuous and not building-centered.

3. *The church of the future must be biblically sound and experientially authentic.* It must know a mysticism joined with action, profound experience wedded to practical exercise. The church must be a genuine community in which wholeness of life grows out of praise to God and fellowship with all men in Christ, without resort to demeaning techniques. The church must grow because of genuine spiritual magnetism, not by religious technology or contentless experience.

4. *The church must live and walk in the Spirit* (Gal. 5:16-26). It must learn in a deepening way the day-by-day guidance and direction of the Spirit of God. The Spirit must be free to produce the fruit and gifts which keep the church healthy and vital.

These are days in which the church must learn to "hang loose," to maintain its independence from the world and its dependence on the Spirit. Today's followers of Christ must learn the full significance of the pattern of the children of Israel in the desert, who went or stopped when the cloud moved or stayed. They must learn to wait upon the Lord, to be sensitive to his leadings and to depend less and less on the arm of flesh. Many local churches could benefit spiritually from applying the principle suggested by Robert Girard in *Brethren, Hang Loose:* "Anything in the church program that cannot be maintained without constant pastoral pressure on the people to be involved should be allowed to die a sure and natural death."[9] Which is another way of saying that the church's life is to be based on the exercise of existing spiritual gifts, not on organizations and programs.

God in Christ has provided marvelous resources for the abundant Christian life. He gives us the strength to serve and endure. My prayer for the church is that she will relearn what the early church knew: These resources are not just for the individual Christian. They are for the community, the church! May God grant that not only isolated believers but *the whole Body of Christ as a community and a people* may walk in the Spirit until it rises triumphant to meet Christ in the air.

In many ways, we Christians today are reliving the New Testament age. These are days of rapid church growth, and yet also of uncertainty, apostasy, threatening persecution and, above all, the expectation of the return of Christ. This was the situation of the early church. First-generation Christians thought Christ would come back. He didn't.

What about Christians at the end of the twentieth century? Like the first Christians, or like believers in A.D. 999, we could be mistaken about the times and seasons. Perhaps Jesus' return is near, perhaps not. In any case, the church is clearly facing difficult days. Many believe that if Christ does not return soon, then some great catastrophe is surely coming.

But dare we hope for a miracle? Is it possible that God in his grace will grant another reprieve in human history, another chance for the church to really be the church? Is this the meaning of the Spirit's new stirrings in our day?

Is it possible that God yet has a great kingdom task for the church to perform?

The church seems impotent before the ecological crisis, for example, or in the face of mindless technology or the worldwide web of political power and intrigue. But the weapons of our warfare are spiritual, not carnal. Using the world's weapons, the church does not stand a chance. But when the church uses God's weapons (Eph. 6:14-17), it is the world which becomes weak.

These are not days for the church to turn inward, curl up in a corner and passively await the end. The world has yet to see what the Spirit can do through the church to establish God's kingdom on earth. God's "new thing" may have a greater beginning *in human history today* than we have thought possible.

In any case, these are days for extreme watchfulness: for alertness to what is happening in the world and for careful attention to God's Word to the church through the Scriptures. And these are days for great expectancy, for God's arm still is not shortened. He is still the God who says, "I will do marvels."

And it is the Lord Jesus who still says to the church: "Watch, therefore. . . ."

NOTES

Introduction

[1]Psalms 40:3; 96:1; 98:1; Ezekiel 11:19; 18:31; 36:36; Isaiah 62:2; 65:17; 66:22; Jeremiah 31:31; 2 Corinthians 5:17; Hebrews 9:15.

[2]For a description of modern Pentecostalism in Latin America and a discussion of the positive aspects of Pentecostalism, see C. Peter Wagner, *Look Out! The Pentecostals Are Coming* (Eastbourne: Coverdale, 1974).

Chapter 1

[1]As I shall subsequently make clear, I am not depreciating theology or the necessity of a proper emphasis on truth. My point here is that neither theology nor structures must be permitted to take priority over the Person of Christ and the new life he offers.

[2]See especially David Mains, *Full Circle* (Waco, Tex.: Word, 1971) and Lawrence Richards, *A New Face for the Church* (Grand Rapids: Zondervan, 1970). Also significant are Donald G. Bloesch, *The Reform of the Church* (Grand Rapids: Eerdmans, 1970), and Gene A. Getz, *Sharpening the Focus of the Church* (Chicago: Moody Press, 1974).

[3]Dietrich Bonhoeffer, *Letters and Papers from Prison*, rev. trans. (London: SCM Press, 1973). These comments of Bonhoeffer are, for my purposes here, merely suggestive. Their inclusion does not imply my full agreement with Bonhoeffer's theology or with his overall view of the church.

Chapter 2

[1]Bonhoeffer, *Letters and Papers.*

[2]Ibid.

[3]Ibid.

[4]Ibid.

[5]E. M. Blaiklock, "Merely, Militantly Christian," *Christianity Today*, 15, No. 16 (May 7, 1971), 6.

[6]Herman Kahn and Anthony J. Wiener, *The Year 2000, A Framework for Speculation on the Next Thirty-Three Years* (London: Macmillan, 1968), p. 189.

[7]Ibid., p. 193.

[8]Ibid., p. 7.

[9]Adolf Harnack, *The Mission and Expansion of Christianity in the First Three Centuries* (New York: Harper Torchbooks, 1962), pp. 19-22.

[10]Kenneth Scott Latourette, *A History of the Expansion of Christianity*

(Exeter: Paternoster Press, 1971). Vol. 1, *The First Five Centuries.*

[11]Merrill C. Tenney, *New Testament Times* (Grand Rapids: Eerdmans, 1965), p. 279.

[12]Noel P. Gist and Sylvia Fleis Fava, *Urban Society*, 5th ed. (New York: Thomas Y. Crowell, 1964), p. 68.

[13]Harvey Cox, *The Secular City* (London: SCM Press, 1966).

[14]Will and Ariel Durant, *The Lessons of History* (New York: Simon and Schuster, 1968), p. 81.

[15]Michael Green, *Evangelism in the Early Church* (London: Hodder and Stoughton, 1973).

[16]Gist and Fava, *Urban Society*, p. 23.

[17]Harnack, *The Mission and Expansion of Christianity*, p. 21.

[18]Ibid., pp. 22-23.

[19]Zbigniew Brzezinski, *Between Two Ages: America's Role in the Technetronic Era* (New York: Viking Press, 1970), p. 111. © 1970 by Zbigniew Brzezinski. Reprinted by permission of the Viking Press.

[20]Latourette, *A History of the Expansion of Christianity.*

[21]Green, *Evangelism in the Early Church.*

[22]Brzezinski, *Between Two Ages*, p. 64. Italics added.

[23]Green, *Evangelism in the Early Church.*

[24]David Snell, "Goom Rodgie's Razzle-Dazzle Soul Rush," *Saturday Review/World*, 1, No. 11 (February 9, 1974), pp. 18-21, 51.

[25]Green, *Evangelism in the Early Church.*

[26]For example, the *Time* cover story, "Astrology and the New Cult of the Occult," March 21, 1969. Within the last two years in Brazil, newsstands have begun increasingly to carry material on astrology, spiritism, mythology, the occult and so forth. A major magazine publisher has come out with a collection, in periodic installments, on classic mythology. And these are being bought, not principally in the unenlightened interior, but in such sophisticated industrial centers as São Paulo and Rio de Janeiro.

[27]Latourette, *A History of the Expansion of Christianity.*

[28]*Time* cover story, January 11, 1971.

[29]Robert J. Blaikie, *"Secular Christianity" and God Who Acts* (London: Hodder and Stoughton, 1970); Francis A. Schaeffer, *The God Who is There* (London: Hodder and Stoughton, 1970). I consider Blaikie's book particularly significant and worthy of more attention than it has received. His contention that the modern predicament in theology traces back to the dualistic methodology of Descartes deserves serious study, as does his criticism of Schaeffer's analysis in *The God Who is There* and *Escape from Reason.* Blaikie is right to insist that a sound biblical theology cannot be built on nonbiblical philosophical presuppositions.

[30]Harnack, *The Mission and Expansion of Christianity*, pp. 1-18.

[31]Donald G. Bloesch, *Wellsprings of Renewal* (Grand Rapids: Eerdmans, 1974).

[32]It is clear that Joel 2:28-32 was not totally fulfilled on the day of Pentecost; not all the signs there recorded have yet occurred. As with many Old Testament prophecies, so here: There was an initial fulfillment (the "first installment") in the New Testament age; there has been some continuing fulfillment throughout history through the Spirit's work through the church; and there will be a final complete and climactic fulfillment in the future. This final fulfillment is, of course, associated in Scripture with the return of Christ.

Chapter 3

[1]The subject of the gospel to the poor is almost totally absent from most contemporary writing on the church, especially evangelical writing. One author who has dealt with the subject, although not in great depth nor sufficiently biblically, is Richard Batey in his *Jesus and the Poor* (New York: Harper & Row, 1972).

[2]John Calvin, *Commentary on a Harmony of the Evangelists, Matthew, Mark, and Luke* (Grand Rapids: Eerdmans, 1957), II, 36.

[3]Walter Rauschenbusch, *Christianity and the Social Crisis* (New York: Hodder and Stoughton, 1907), p. 82.

[4]Bruce Kendrick, *Come Out the Wilderness* (London: Fontana, 1966), p. 31.

[5]David L. McKenna, ed., *The Urban Crisis* (Grand Rapids: Zondervan, 1969), p. 138.

[6]Gibson Winter, *The Suburban Captivity of the Churches* (London: Macmillan, 1962), p. 140.

[7]Ernest Campbell, *Christian Manifesto* (New York: Harper & Row, 1970), p. 9.

[8]Leighton Ford, *The Christian Persuader* (London: Hodder and Stoughton, 1969).

[9]Quoted in H. Richard Niebuhr, *The Social Sources of Denominationalism* (Cleveland: World, 1957), p. 29. See also Eric Hoffer, *The True Believer* (London: Harper & Row, 1951), pp. 20–48.

[10]Ernst Troeltsch, *The Social Teaching of the Christian Churches*, trans. Olive Wyon (London: George Allen and Unwin Ltd., 1956), I, 39.

[11]John Wesley, *The Works of John Wesley* (Grand Rapids: Zondervan, n.d.), III, 445.

[12]Donald McGavran, *The Bridges of God* (London: World Dominion Press, 1955).

[13]Donald McGavran, *Understanding Church Growth* (Grand Rapids: Eerdmans, 1970), p. 19.

[14]William R. Read, *New Patterns of Church Growth in Brazil* (Grand Rapids: Eerdmans, 1965), p. 225.

[15]Niebuhr, *The Social Sources of Denominationalism*, pp. 54, 28.

[16]This is a fundamental but wrong and essentially worldly assumption that nearly everyone starts with when Christian witness to the poor is considered.

[17]Evangelism among the poor is complicated by the fact that the poor often represent one or more distinct subcultures within the dominant culture of a society. Thus the problem of cross-cultural communication comes into play and must be considered. See, in this regard, Charles H. Kraft, "North America's Cultural Challenge," and Ralph D. Winter, "Existing Churches: Means or Ends?" both in *Christianity Today*, 16, No. 8 (January 19, 1973), 6-8 and 10-13. The first step toward cross-cultural relevance, however, is the recovery of the biblical concept of the church. See Richards, *A New Face for the Church*, pp. 235-82, for suggestions on ministering to the poor.

[18]Niebuhr, *The Social Sources of Denominationalism*, p. 34.

[19]Hendrick Hart, "The Institutional Church in Biblical Perspective: Cultus and Covenant," in *Will All the King's Men . . .* (Toronto: Wedge Publishing Foundation, 1972), p. 30.

[20]Bloesch, *The Reform of the Church*, p. 113; John Howard Yoder, "The Fullness of Christ, Perspectives on Ministries in Renewal," *Concern*, No. 17 (February, 1969), pp. 33-93. While the reformers affirmed "the priesthood of all believers," they applied this emphasis primarily to soteriology (all may approach God directly) rather than ecclesiology (all believers are ministers in the church and priests to each other).

[21]Roland H. Bainton, *The Reformation of the Sixteenth Century* (London: Hodder and Stoughton, 1963).

[22]Niebuhr, *The Social Sources of Denominationalism*, p. 39.

[23]Bainton, *The Reformation of the Sixteenth Century*.

[24]There are several points of contact between the approach advocated in this book and the thinking of such groups as the Anabaptists, Quakers, and Plymouth Brethren. I hold that these groups took much of their dynamic from their rediscovery of basic biblical truths about the church, even while they mixed these with other ideas which were less biblical. Because of the historically conditioned nature of each of these groups—the "cultural factor"—no one of them (or even the early church, for that matter) may be taken as a perfect model for the church today. This is not what I propose in this book, nor is this book merely a restate-

ment of the views of earlier reform movements. Rather it is a call for serious reflection on the problem of church structure and for the fresh application of basic biblical concepts of the church to our age.

Chapter 4

[1]Oscar Cullmann suggests that in John 2:12-22 the author "understands the clearing of the Temple as signifying that the *Temple worship* itself is replaced by the person of Christ." Christ himself is the center of worship; the temple has thus lost this centrality. Similarly, "When Jesus said after the destruction of the Temple he would raise up a Temple in 3 days (= in a short space of time) . . . it can only refer to the community of disciples." Oscar Cullmann, *Early Christian Worship* (London: SCM Press 1969), pp. 72-73; compare p. 117.

[2]"It is to be remembered . . . that if the work of man and the history of man are taken up by God and recapitulated in the glorified Christ, that is definitely not because they are valid, not because they make a positive contribution to improve that which God has willed, but because, in his love, God saves man *with* his works. It is by grace that he transforms evil into good, and wills indeed to take into account what man has done. The new creation is not superior to the first by the addition of the work and history of man, but by a new achievement of the love of God." Jacques Ellul, *False Presence of the Kingdom*, trans. C. Edward Hopkin (New York: Seabury Press, 1972), p. 29.

[3]The typological nature of the Davidic dynasty is particularly clear in God's promise that he would establish from David's line an eternal kingdom (2 Sam. 7:1-29 and 1 Chron. 17:10-27). Although there is a primary reference here to Solomon, the passage is clearly messianic.

[4]For example, in Micah 1:2; Habakkuk 2:20; Psalms 11:4; 18:6.

[5]See chapter 8.

[6]But what about the Jewish synagogue? Wasn't it a building? Didn't the early Christians meet there? Wasn't it Paul's intention that the synagogues become centers of Christian worship?

The synagogue was in the first place a community of Jews; only secondarily did the term come to mean a building. There were hundreds of synagogue communities, as well as buildings, throughout the Roman Empire, and to these Paul went first with the gospel. Doubtless Paul would have liked to have seen these synagogue buildings converted into Christian centers, but, in the providence of God, that did not happen. The synagogues never became Christian churches, so far as we know, and within thirty years or so of the birth of the church the Christians found "the door into the synagogue . . . slammed in their faces" (Green,

Evangelism in the Early Church).

What Paul planted was not buildings—significantly, he built no physical synagogues—but synagogue-type *communities*. As Ralph Winter notes, he "established brand new synagogue-type fellowships of believers as the basic unit of his missionary activity. The first structure in the New Testament scene is thus what is often called the *New Testament Church*. It was essentially built along Jewish synagogue lines, embracing the community of the faithful in any given place" (Ralph D. Winter, "The Two Structures of God's Redemptive Mission," *Missiology*, 2, No. 1 [January, 1974], 122).

It is interesting that the early Christians normally called themselves the *ecclesia* rather than the *synagogue*. Both Greek words can be translated *assembly* (compare Jas. 2:2, where *assembly* in the Greek is *synagogue*), and, grammatically, *synagogue* would have been an appropriate title for the church. The early church's preference for *ecclesia* suggests a desire to clearly distinguish the Christian community from the Jewish synagogue. (See Harnack, *The Mission and Expansion of Christianity*, pp. 407-08.)

The synagogue provided a vital bridge for the gospel from Palestine to the rest of the Roman Empire and from the Jews to the Gentiles. But it was a bridge that, once crossed, was left behind. The early church copied the synagogue *as a pattern of community*, but apparently never *as a building*.

[7]John F Havlik, *People-Centered Evangelism* (Nashville: Broadman Press, 1971), p 47

Chapter 5

[1]Walter Oetting, *The Church of the Catacombs* (London: Concordia, 1964), p. 25.

[2]It is true that there is a significant trend today toward greater flexibility in the construction of buildings. This can be significant for the church. Where some form of physical facilities becomes necessary, high priority should be given to flexibility and multifunctionality. See Alvin Toffler, *Future Shock* (London: Bodley Head, 1970).

[3]Lawrence Carter, *Cant You Here Me Calling?* (New York: Seabury Press, 1969), p. 131

[4]See chapter 7

[5]In the first century, Christians often met in the private homes of people of means who had been converted. Although by far the majority of Christians in the early church were from the poorer classes, from the beginning there was also a scattering of wealthy converts. Their spacious

homes often provided ample room for relatively large gatherings. Along this line, see Michael Green's scholarly book, *Evangelism in the Early Church.*

[6]Church groups I know of have met in schools, store fronts and YMCA facilities. One creative, and apparently Spirit-led, solution to this problem of a place for large-group worship is related in David Mains, *Full Circle.*

[7]Peter Wagner suggests that "the rule of thumb for churches that have been fired with a vision for a lost world in need of Christ is a minimum of 50 percent of the church budget for missions. They spend at least as much on reaching others for Christ as they spend on their own needs." C. Peter Wagner, *Stop the World, I Want to Get On* (Glendale, Cal.: Regal, 1974), p. 66.

[8]Chuck Smith and Hugh Steven, *The Reproducers* (Glendale, Cal.: Regal, 1972), pp. 55-63.

[9]Juan Carlos Ortiz, in an interview on July 19, 1974, during the International Congress on World Evangelization in Lausanne, Switzerland.

Chapter 7

[1]Keith Miller, *The Taste of New Wine* (Hemel Hempstead: Word, 1965).

[2]George A. Buttrick, ed., *The Interpreter's Bible* (New York: Abingdon Press, 1953), X, 425. Italics added.

[3]Hendrik Kraemer, *A Theology of the Laity* (Guildford: Lutterworth Press, 1958).

[4]In my own upbringing, the religious highpoint was always the "altar service" which commonly followed the worship service if an "altar call" had been given and responded to. From a few minutes to more than an hour might be given to singing and hearing the testimonies of those who had just found spiritual victory. Even though, on mature reflection, one may see certain negative aspects to the traditional altar call and altar service, still (at least in my own experience) a deep, if fleeting, spiritual communal reality was tasted there which is unforgettable. That very reality today convinces me all the more of the need for more viable and workable structures of common life which allow this reality to be experienced, not as an abnormal spiritual "high" but as the normal life of the church.

[5]Robert Coleman, *The Master Plan of Evangelism* (Westwood, N.J.:Fleming H. Revell, 1963), p. 43

[6]Daniel J. Fleming, *Living as Comrades* (New York: Agricultural Missions, 1950), p. 19.

[7]I go into more detail about basic considerations for church structure in

chapter 12.

[8]Quoted in Os Guinness, *The Dust of Death* (London: Inter-Varsity Press, 1971), p. 211.

[9]Robert Raines, *New Life in the Church* (New York: Harper & Row, 1961), p. 71.

[10]George W. Webber, *The Congregation in Mission* (New York: Abingdon Press, 1964), p. 81.

Chapter 8

[1]It may be that in the statement "A man leaves his father and his mother and cleaves to his wife, and they become one flesh" (Gen. 2:24) is implied an analogy to a people being called out from the nations to be one people for God.

[2]God still has a plan, of course, for the biological or racial Israel, for the Jews are still his people. In the end time the Jews and the church will be integrated into one faithful people of God (Rom. 11:1-36).

[3]Gerhard Kittel, ed., *Theological Dictionary of the New Testament,* trans. Geoffrey W. Bromiley (Grand Rapids: Eerdmans, 1967), IV, 32.

[4]Ibid., p. 35.

[5]Ibid., p. 54.

[6]James Leo Garrett, Jr., ed., *The Concept of the Believers' Church* (Scottdale, Penn.: Herald Press, 1969), p. 258.

[7]Ibid., pp. 259-60.

[8]Jacques Ellul, *The Meaning of the City,* trans. Dennis Pardee (Grand Rapids: Eerdmans, 1970), pp. 5-6, 77.

[9]Jess Moody, *A Drink at Joel's Place* (Waco, Tex.: Word, 1967), pp. 22, 17.

[10]Garrett, *The Concept of the Believers' Church,* p. 274. Italics added.

[11]Is it possible there is a connection between the camp meeting movement and the social involvement of many nineteenth-century revivalists? I suspect there is, for the camp meeting provided a significant platform for social reformers and a large, sympathetic audience. See Timothy Smith, *Revivalism and Social Reform* (Nashville: Abingdon Press, 1957).

[12]Some of the Psalms recount in historical sequence God's dealings with his people. These psalms were probably used liturgically. Why shouldn't the church today hold periodic "covenant celebrations," picking up where these psalms leave off and recounting God's dealings down through church history? Certainly the acts of God are discernible in various movements and men, and these can legitimately be celebrated, giving glory to God. For one attempt somewhat along this line, see H. R. Rookmaaker, *Modern Art and the Death of a Culture* (London: Inter-

Varsity Press, 1970), pp. 250–52.

Chapter 9

[1]Philip Morrison, "The Mind of the Machine," *Technology Review*, January, 1973, p. 17.

[2]Kittel, *Theological Dictionary of the New Testament*, IV, 948-60. For a good study of the biblical usage of *nous*, see Mildred B. Wynkoop, *A Theology of Love* (Kansas City, Mo.: Beacon Hill Press of Kansas City, 1972), pp. 132-35.

[3]Wynkoop, *A Theology of Love*, p. 121.

[4]Kahn and Wiener, *The Year 2000*, pp. 346-47.

[5]Toffler, *Future Shock*.

[6]Jacques Ellul, *To Will and To Do*, trans. C. Edward Hopkin (Philadelphia: Pilgrim Press, 1969), p. 185.

[7]Ibid., p. 190.

[8]B. F. Skinner, *Beyond Freedom and Dignity* (London: Cape, 1972).

[9]Francis A. Schaeffer, *True Spirituality* (London: Hodder and Stoughton, 1972).

[10]George Orwell, *1984* (London: Secker and Warburg, 1949).

[11]Toffler, *Future Shock*.

[12]John Kenneth Galbraith, *The New Industrial State*, rev. ed. (London: Deutsch, 1972).

[13]Gary Henley, *The Quiet Revolution* (Carol Stream, Ill.: Creation House, 1970), pp. 46-47.

[14]See chapter 12.

Chapter 10

[1]Paul Verghese, "A Sacramental Humanism," in Alan Geyer and Dean Peerman, eds., *Theological Crossings* (Grand Rapids: Eerdmans, 1971), pp. 137-45.

[2]Mains, *Full Circle*, p. 62.

[3]Ibid., p. 63.

[4]Elizabeth O'Connor, *Eighth Day of Creation* (Waco, Tex.: Word, 1971), pp. 42-43.

[5]Ray C. Stedman, *Body Life* (Glendale, Cal.: Regal, 1972); Robert C. Girard, *Brethren, Hang Loose!* (Grand Rapids: Zondervan, 1972).

[6]C. Peter Wagner, *Frontiers in Missionary Strategy* (Chicago: Moody Press, 1971); *Stop the World, I Want to Get On.*

Chapter 11

[1]Donald G. Bloesch, *The Evangelical Renaissance* (London: Hodder and

Stoughton, 1974).

[2]Vinson Synan, *The Holiness-Pentecostal Movement* (Grand Rapids: Eerdmans, 1971), p. 42. By 1891, "weekday meetings for the promotion of holiness" patterned after Phoebe Palmer's famous "Tuesday Meetings" numbered over 350

[3]W. Stanford Reid, "The Grass-Roots Reformation," *Christianity Today,* 15, No. 2 (October 23, 1970), 62-64

[4]Elton Trueblood, *The Incendiary Fellowship* (New York: Harper & Row, 1967), p. 70.

[5]Raines, *New Life in the Church,* p. 70.

[6]Moody, *A Drink at Joel's Place,* p. 24

[7]George W. Webber, *God's Colony in Man's World* (New York: Abingdon Press, 1960), and *The Congregation in Mission.*

[8]Webber, *The Congregation in Mission,* p. 121.

[9]Ibid.

[10]Webber, *God's Colony in Man's World,* pp. 58-59. Italics added.

[11]Ibid., p. 58.

[12]Ibid.

[13]Webber, *The Congregation in Mission,* p. 131.

[14]Ibid., p. 122.

[15]Ibid., p. 82.

[16]Robert Coleman, *Dry Bones Can Live Again* (Old Tappan, N.J.: Fleming H. Revell, 1969), p. 70.

[17]Webber, *The Congregation in Mission,* pp. 163-64.

[18]Ibid.

[19]John Wesley, "A Plain Account of the People Called Methodists," in *Works,* VIII, 254.

Chapter 12

[1]Donald A. McGavran, "The Dimensions of World Evangelization." Issue Strategy Paper prepared for the International Congress on World Evangelization, Lausanne, Switzerland, July 16-25, 1974.

[2]K. L. Schmidt comments that in the attempt "to try to understand the antithesis between an empirical Church and an ideal" in the post-apostolic church "there arises an awareness of the twofold nature of the Church as the Church militant and the Church triumphant. Such speculations introduce a distinctive ambiguity into statements concerning the Church. This is equally true of both the Greek and the Latin fathers. The greatest of them, Augustine, whose comprehensive thinking set the Church in the centre of Roman Catholic life and thought, is the very one in whom the relation between the empirical and the ideal Church is not

made clear. If genuinely Gnostic speculation was held at bay, speculation still established itself in the form of Platonism. Protestantism, with its distinction between the invisible and the visible Church, has its own share in this unrealistic Platonism."

Schmidt says further that the church "as the assembly of God in Christ is not invisible on the one side and visible on the other. The Christian community, which as the individual congregation represents the whole body, is just as visible and corporeal as the individual man. .. If Luther distinguished between the invisible and the visible Church, . . . he did so without accepting the Platonism of his successors." Kittel, *Theological Dictionary of the New Testament,* III, 533-34.

[3]I recognize there is a problem with the word *institution* for any "established practice, law, or custom" may be considered an institution (*Webster's New Practical Dictionary*). In this sense baptism and the Lord's Supper, for instance, may be thought of as institutions, and it is difficult to make a distinction between *institution* and *church.* But I am here using *institution* in the more restricted (and more popular) sense of "an established society or corporation"; in other words, as a formally structured organization, whether this structuring has come about by law, a constituting assembly or merely accumulated tradition I am aware that some prefer to use the phrase *institutional church* to describe what I here refer to as *community,* but this is not the sense in which I am using the phrase.

[4]The same cosmic-historical perspective is evident throughout Scripture. All the promises of cosmic restoration in the Old Testament prophets apply here, reaching their climax in Isaiah. In the New Testament the essential message of the book of Revelation is the uniting of all things under the lordship of Christ. And Isaiah, Peter and John speak of a new heaven and a new earth (Is. 65:17; 66:22; 2 Pet. 3:13; Rev. 21:1).

[5]Ephesians 1:10; 2 Corinthians 5:17-21, Romans 8:21 The Greek word "to unite" or "to gather together" in Ephesians 1:10 comes from the word for "head." The idea of Christ as the head of the church and of all things (for example, in Eph. 1:22) naturally suggests the thought of uniting all things under the headship of Christ, and this accounts for Paul's using the rather uncommon word "to unite, to bring under proper headship" in Ephesians 1:10. See Kittel, *Theological Dictionary of the New Testament,* III, 681-82.

[6]1 Corinthians 8:6; 15:28; Ephesians 1:22; 3:9; 4:10; Colossians 1:17-20; compare Hebrews 1:2-3; 2:8-10.

[7]Francis A. Schaeffer, *The God Who Is There,* p. 152; *Pollution and the Death of Man* (London: Hodder and Stoughton, 1972). See also

George Eldon Ladd, *Jesus and the Kingdom* (London: SPCK, 1966).

[8]Peter Beyerhaus, "World Evangelization and the Kingdom of God." Biblical Foundation Paper prepared for the International Congress on World Evangelization, Lausanne, Switzerland, July 16-25, 1974.

[9]Clark H. Pinnock, "The New Pentecostalism: Reflections by a Well-Wisher," *Christianity Today*, 17, No. 24 (September 14, 1973), 6.

[10]Bloesch, *The Reform of the Church*, p. 112.

[11]Hans Küng, *Structures of the Church*, trans. Salvator Attanasio (London: Burns and Oates, 1964), p. 12.

[12]1 Peter 4:10; compare Ephesians 3:10. In the Greek the word translated "manifold" (*poikilos*) often has the sense of "many-colored," as in the variety of colors in flowers or clothing. W. Robertson Nicoll, ed., *The Expositor's Greek Testament* (Grand Rapids: Eerdmans, 1961), III, 309.

[13]Hans Küng similarly defines the church as "the People of God . . . the community of the faithful"; "the community of the new people of God called out and called together." *Structures of the Church*, pp. x, 11. This definition is in harmony also with the etymological meaning of the New Testament word for church, *ekklesia*—a called-out and called-together assembly.

[14]This is the traditional Roman Catholic view, but many Protestant groups also tend in this direction, with varying degrees of intensity and self-consciousness.

[15]Francis A. Schaeffer suggests eight biblical norms for church structure in *The Church at the End of the 20th Century* (London: Norfold Press, 1970), pp. 59–67. Although these suggestions go somewhat beyond what I present here and put less emphasis on spiritual gifts, they are not in conflict with the position of this chapter.

[16]That the functions of deacon, elder and bishop were associated with spiritual gifts is suggested by such passages as Acts 20:28; 21:8; 1 Timothy 4:14; 1 Peter 5:1; 2 John 1. The *Didache* also suggests this connection between gifts and leadership functions.

[17]The ministry of the first "deacons" (Acts 8) and of Paul and Barnabas as missionary apostles (Acts 13:1-3) was recognized formally by the church; the evangelistic ministry of Philip and the apostolic ministry of Apollos seem to have become recognized informally as a result of their effectiveness.

[18]See George Peters, *Saturation Evangelism* (Grand Rapids: Zondervan, 1970), p. 33.

[19]Green, *Evangelism in the Early Church.*

[20]Dean M. Kelley, *Why Conservative Churches Are Growing* (New York: Harper & Row, 1972), p. 86.

Chapter 13

[1]Carl F. H. Henry, *A Plea for Evangelical Demonstration* (Grand Rapids: Baker, 1971), p. 31.

[2]Maldwyn Edwards, *John Wesley and the Eighteenth Century* (London: Epworth Press, 1955), pp. 82ff.

[3]Maldwyn Edwards gives an excellent summary of Wesley's efforts along this line in *John Wesley and the Eighteenth Century*. See also Mildred Wynkoop's *A Theology of Love* (an important recent contribution to understanding Wesley), pp. 58-64.

[4]John Wesley, *Journal* (London: Epworth Press, 1938), II, 167.

[5]Ibid., p. 172.

[6]Leslie R. Marston, *From Age to Age a Living Witness, a Historical Interpretation of Free Methodism's First Century* (Winona Lake, Ind.: Light and Life Press, 1960), p. 66.

[7]Quoted in John Stott, *One People* (London: Falcon, 1969).

[8]See, for example, the discussion in H. Richard Niebuhr, *The Kingdom of God in America* (London: Harper Torchbooks, 1959), pp. 205–06.

[9]Charles Wesley wrote over 6,000 hymns. Having gone through a good number of them, however, I would classify only hundreds as "singable." Still, a remarkable achievement!

Chapter 14

[1]Alvin Toffler, *Future Shock.*

[2]Ibid.

[3]Ben H. Bagdikian, *The Information Machines: Their Impact on Men and the Media* (New York: Harper & Row, 1971), p. 287.

[4]Arnold Toynbee, *Change and Habit, The Challenge of Our Time* (London: Oxford Univ. Press, 1966), p. 29.

[5]Jacques Ellul, *The Technological Society*, trans. John Wilkerson (London: Cape, 1965).

[6]Toffler, *Future Shock.*

[7]Toffler (citing Max Weber) reminds us that bureaucracy, as an organizational form, appeared with the rise of industrialism, and suggests that it is passing away as many societies move into a post-industrial phase (*Future Shock*). If this is true, it may be highly significant for denominational and other ecclesiastical organizations, and perhaps suggest even a "post-denominational" phase for the church.

[8]Francis A. Schaeffer, *The Church before the Watching World* (London: Inter-Varsity Press, 1972), p. 62.

[9]Robert C. Girard, *Brethren, Hang Loose!*, p. 73.